Hugo Grotius's *On Public Partnership with Unbelievers*
(*De societate publica cum infidelibus*)

Mini-Monographs in Medieval and Early Modern Studies

VOLUME 5

The titles published in this series are listed at *brill.com/mini*

Hugo Grotius's
On Public Partnership with Unbelievers
(*De societate publica cum infidelibus*)

Introduction, Transcription and English Translation

Edited by

Diederik Burgersdijk
Henk Nellen
Marc de Wilde

BRILL

LEIDEN | BOSTON

Cover illustration: Jan van Ravesteyn, Portrait of Hugo Grotius at the age of sixteen. Panel, diameter 31 cm. Frits Lugt Collection, Fondation Custodia, Parijs, inv. 175.

The Library of Congress Cataloging-in-Publication Data is available online at https://catalog.loc.gov

Typeface for the Latin, Greek, and Cyrillic scripts: "Brill". See and download: brill.com/brill-typeface.

ISSN 2949-8686
ISBN 978-90-04-74458-5 (paperback)
ISBN 978-90-04-74459-2 (e-book)
DOI 10.1163/9789004744592

This book is printed on acid-free paper and produced in a sustainable manner.

Contents

Acknowledgements

This edition of Hugo Grotius's *On Public Partnership with Unbelievers* (*De societate publica cum infidelibus*) was first published in *Grotiana* 45 (1) (2024), 33–157. We are grateful to the editors of *Grotiana*, Hans Blom and Mark Somos, for kindly granting permission to republish this edition. We are also indebted to two anonymous reviewers for their detailed comments and suggestions for improving the text. Our thanks extend to Harmen Luth for his assistance in preparing the indices for this edition. In addition, we like to thank our editors at Brill, Alessandra Giliberto, Helena Schöb and Petra Stiglmayer, for their valuable advice. We also thank the Leiden University Library for kindly granting permission for the publication of pictures of Grotius's manuscript. Finally, we thank the director of the Foundation Custodia, Stijn Alsteens, for allowing us to use the beautiful portrait of Hugo Grotius at the age of sixteen by Jan van Ravesteyn, which is part of the Frits Lugt Collection in Paris, for the cover of our book. Henk Nellen prepared the transcription of the Latin text, Diederik Burgersdijk translated it into English, and Marc de Wilde wrote the introduction. As the authors constantly discussed their work with each other, it should be seen as the product of collaborative research. The introduction builds on arguments that were first presented in Marc de Wilde, 'Hugo de Groots *De societate publica cum infidelibus*: Pleidooi voor tolerantie of rechtvaardiging van kolonialisme', in *De achterkant van Minerva: Opstellen aangeboden aan prof. Kees Cappon ter gelegenheid van zijn afscheid van de Universiteit van Amsterdam*, ed. by Gustaaf van Nifterik, Joke de Vries and Marc de Wilde (Amsterdam: 2019), pp. 115–128, translated as 'Hugo Grotius's *De Societate publica cum infidelibus*: Justifying Overseas Expansionism or Religious Toleration', *Tijdschrift voor rechtsgeschiedenis*, 88 (2020), 422–439.

Introduction and Analysis

1 Introduction

The Leiden University Library has an important collection of manuscripts of the Dutch humanist and international lawyer Hugo Grotius (1583–1645). Apart from the famous manuscript of *De iure praedae* (*On the Law of Prize and Booty*), it possesses a collection of legal and political manuscripts, which includes an unpublished autograph, entitled *De societate publica cum infidelibus*, 'On Public Partnership with Unbelievers'.[1] The existence of *De societate* has been known since 1864, when it was discovered by the bibliographer Pieter Anton Tiele during preparations for an auction of a large collection of Grotius's manuscripts and working papers.[2] However, it was largely ignored by scholars until Peter Borschberg described it in an article published in 1998.[3] Borschberg identified *De societate* as an early work of Grotius, probably written in the first decade of the seventeenth century. Analyzing the text and its sources, he concluded that *De societate* was written in connection with *De iure praedae*—a title that was posthumously given to a work to which Grotius himself referred as *De rebus Indicis* (*On Indian Affairs*).[4] As Borschberg explained, in both treatises, Grotius's aim was to defend the Dutch policies of treaty and alliance-making in the East Indies, and more particularly, the right of the Dutch East India Company (VOC) to enter into alliances with non-Christian rulers that were aimed against the Spaniards and Portuguese.[5]

---

1 Leiden University Library, MS Cod. BPL 922 Ie, fol. 314–318. The manuscript is available online at: https://digitalcollections.universiteitleiden.nl/view/item/936830#page/51/mode/1up. BPL 922 I contains five manuscripts of Grotius: (a) *Commentarius in theses XI* (fol. 276–286), (b) *Theses sive quaestiones LVI* (fol. 287–292), (c) *Commentarius de bello ob libertatem eligendo* (fol. 293–307), (d) *Observationes iuridicae contra pacem cum archiduce Alberto ineundam, non autographae* (fol. 308–313), and (e) *De societate publica cum infidelibus* (fol. 314–318).

2 *Catalogue de manuscrits autographes de Hugo Grotius dont la vente a eu lieu à la Haye le 15 novembre 1864 sous la direction et au domicile de Martinus Nijhoff*, ed. by W.J.M. van Eysinga and L.J. Noordhoff (The Hague: Martinus Nijhoff, 1952), p. 27 (lot. 78).

3 Peter Borschberg, 'De societate publica cum infidelibus: Ein Frühwerk von Hugo Grotius', *Zeitschrift der Savigny-Stiftung für Rechtsgeschichte: Romanistische Abteilung*, 115 (1998), 355–393.

4 Letter of Hugo Grotius to Georg Lingelsheim, 1 November 1606, in Hugo Grotius, *Briefwisseling van Hugo Grotius*, ed. by P.C. Molhuysen (The Hague: Martinus Nijhoff, 1928), vol. 1, p. 72 (no. 86). Henceforth referred to as BW.

5 Borschberg, 'De societate', p. 356.

 | DOI:10.1163/9789004744592_002

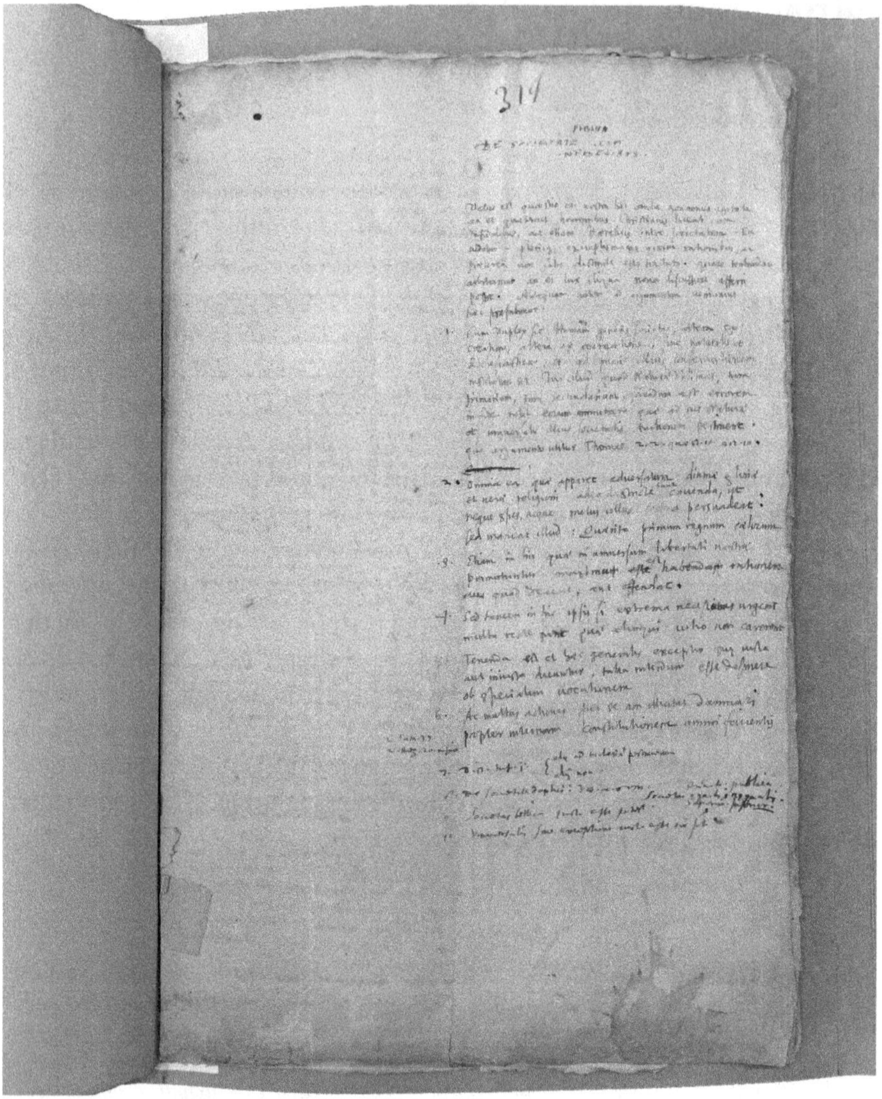

FIGURE 1 First page of *De societate publica cum infidelibus*, written in the hand of Grotius. The page contains the title, followed by a short introduction and ten premises. Leiden University Library, MS BPL 922 Ie, fol. 314^{r}.

Borschberg's thorough analysis of *De societate* has remained the standard interpretation in the literature. As no transcription or translation of *De societate* was available, scholars tended to consult Borschberg's analysis of the text, rather than the text itself. However, in our view, there are several reasons why it is valuable for jurists and historians to study the original text of *De societate*. First of all, Grotius's treatise is important for understanding his ideas about legal relations between Christians and non-Christians (e.g., Jews and Muslims). In *De societate*, Grotius explains what kinds of public and private partnerships with non-Christians are lawful, both in the international context (e.g., treaties and alliances with non-Christian rulers) *and* in the domestic context (e.g., legal relations with non-Christian minorities residing in Christian states). Secondly, *De societate* gives important insights into Grotius's ideas about the relationship between natural law and Christian law and, more particularly, the role of natural law as a source of universal legal norms which apply across cultural and religious boundaries. For instance, in his treatise, Grotius explains that partnerships between Christians and non-Christians are generally permissible under natural law, while they should also be limited and regulated on the basis of Christian law. And finally, *De societate* may contribute to a better understanding of the connection between Grotius's earlier and later writings. As we will show in this introduction, there are many parallels between *De societate* and some of Grotius's other writings, notably *De iure praedae*, the *Remonstrantie* (*Remonstrance*, 1615), and *De iure belli ac pacis* (*On the Law of War and Peace*, 1625).[6] Studying *De societate* may thus contribute to a better understanding of how Grotius's ideas about legal relations between Christians and non-Christians developed over time.[7] For these reasons, we have decided to publish the first complete transcription and English translation of Grotius's text.

In recent years, there has been increasing attention for Grotius's role as legal advisor of the Dutch East India Company.[8] The fact that the 'founding father

6 We have used the following editions: Hugo Grotius, *De iure praedae commentarius*, ed. by H.G. Hamaker (The Hague: Martinus Nijhoff, 1868), trans. as Hugo Grotius, *Commentary on the Law of Prize and Booty*, ed. by Martine van Ittersum, trans. by Gwladys L. Williams (Indianapolis: Liberty Fund, 2006), henceforth referred to as *IPC*; Hugo Grotius, *Remonstrantie of 1615: Facsimile, Transliteration, Modern Translations and Analysis*, ed. by David Kromhout and Adri K. Offenberg, trans. by Cis van Heerum (Leiden: Brill, 2019), henceforth referred to as *Remonstrantie*; and Hugo Grotius, *De iure belli ac pacis libri tres*, ed. by B.J.A de Kanter-Van Hettinga Tromp, annot. by F. Feenstra, C.E. Persenaire, and E. Arps-de Wilde (Aalen: Scientia Verlag, 1993), trans. as Hugo Grotius, *De jure belli ac pacis libri tres*, ed. by James Brown Scott, trans. by Francis W. Kelsey (Oxford: Clarendon Press), vol. 2: translation (trans. based on the Blaeu edition of 1646), henceforth referred to as *IBP*.

7 Orazio Condorelli, 'Grotius's Doctrine of Alliances with Infidels and the Idea of Respublica Christiana', *Grotiana*, 41 (2020), 13–39 (p. 24).

8 See, *inter alia*, Peter Borschberg, 'Hugo Grotius and the East Indies', in *The Cambridge Companion to Hugo Grotius*, ed. by Randall Lesaffer and Janne Nijman (Cambridge: Cambridge University Press, 2021), pp. 65–90; Peter Borschberg, *Hugo Grotius, the Portuguese and Free Trade in the East Indies* (Singapore: NUS Press, 2011); Martine van Ittersum, 'The Long Good-

of modern international law' had also been active as VOC advisor has attracted the attention of jurists and historians who seek to understand how his ideas about international law related to his defense of Dutch empire-building in Asia and the East Indies. This has led to a renewed interest in Grotius's *De societate*: as a renowned historian puts it, *De societate* shows that Grotius was 'himself in the forefront of the Dutch attempts in these years to build a network of alliances with infidels against the Portuguese'.[9] Like Borschberg, historians such as Richard Tuck and Martine van Ittersum believe that Grotius wrote *De societate* alongside *De iure praedae* to demonstrate that the VOC's alliances with non-Christian rulers in the East Indies were justified by the law of nature.[10] As is well known, Grotius had written *De iure praedae* at the request of the Amsterdam Chamber of the VOC to defend the seizure of a Portuguese vessel, the *Santa Catarina*, off the coast of Johor (present-day Singapore).[11] As Grotius argued in his treatise, the VOC had entered into an alliance with the (Muslim) king of Johor on behalf of the Dutch Estates General; the VOC had thereby obtained access to local trade in exchange for offering the king and his people military protection. When the Portuguese had attacked Johor, the Dutch had provided military assistance to their ally and seized the Santa Catarina.[12] For Grotius, the alliance with the king of Johor thus served as an important argument for justifying the seizure of the Santa Catarina as a 'just prize' taken in a 'public war'.[13]

---

bye: Hugo Grotius' Justification of Dutch Expansion Overseas', *History of European Ideas*, 36 (4) (2010), 386–411; Martine van Ittersum, *Profit and Principle: Hugo Grotius, Natural Rights Theories and the Rise of Dutch Power in the East Indies (1595–1615)* (Leiden: Brill, 2006); Edward Keene, *Beyond the Anarchical Society: Grotius, Colonialism and Order in World Politics* (Cambridge: Cambridge University Press, 2002); Eric Wilson, *Savage Republic: De Indis of Hugo Grotius, Republicanism and Dutch Hegemony within the Early-Modern World System (c. 1600–1619)* (Leiden: Brill, 2008); Henk Nellen, 'Hugo Grotius over kaapvaart en commerciële expansie', *Leidschrift*, 26 (2011), 59–73.

9 Richard Tuck, 'Alliances with Infidels in the European Imperial Expansion', in *Empire and Modern Political Thought*, ed. by Sankar Muthu (Cambridge: Cambridge University Press, 2012), pp. 61–83 (p. 75).

10 Ibid., p. 75 and Van Ittersum, *Profit and Principle*, pp. 49–50.

11 As early as 1868, the Dutch historian Robert Fruin demonstrated that Grotius had been commissioned by the VOC to write a treatise to defend the seizure of the *Santa Catarina*. Fruin believed that Grotius wrote *De iure praedae* primarily to convince Mennonite shareholders of the VOC of the legitimacy of its legal claims to the Portuguese vessel. An English translation of Fruin's seminal article was published in 1925 under the title 'An Unpublished Work of Hugo Grotius', *Bibliotheca Visseriana*, 5 (1925), 3–71. For a critical discussion of Fruin's thesis and the circumstances which led Grotius to write *De iure praedae*, see Van Ittersum, *Profit and Principle*, pp. 105–188.

12 *IPC*, ed. Hamaker, pp. 202–203, ed. Van Ittersum, pp. 296–297.

13 *IPC*, ed. Hamaker, p. 297, ed. Van Ittersum, p. 432.

As Martine van Ittersum and Richard Tuck have pointed out, Grotius's claims in *De iure praedae* regarding the right of the Dutch to enter into military alliances with non-Christian rulers such as the king of Johor were not uncontroversial.[14] The traditional view was that military alliances with non-Christians were permissible only in case of self-defense: a Christian nation could thus use the aid of non-Christian allies to protect itself from (impending) attack, but only in case of 'imminent necessity', not otherwise.[15] By contrast, Grotius claimed that the Dutch had a right to wage a public war against another Christian nation (e.g., the Portuguese) on behalf of a non-Christian ally (e.g., the king of Johor), even if they were not themselves attacked. He also maintained that they had seized the Santa Catarina on behalf of the king of Johor, who had ceded his right to the prize to the VOC in gratitude of its assistance.[16] In the eyes of Grotius's contemporaries, these were startling claims, as they implied that the Dutch had more in common with 'infidels' than with their fellow-Christians. According to Van Ittersum, it is therefore likely that Grotius wrote *De societate* to support the conclusions he had presented in *De iure praedae*: his aim was to demonstrate that the right to enter into military alliances with non-Christians originated from natural law, and more specifically, from the natural law of non-offensiveness (i.e., the duty not to harm others without cause), which applied irrespective of religious belief. Like Borschberg and Tuck, Van Ittersum emphasizes the similarities between *De iure praedae* and *De societate*: in both texts, Grotius concluded that Christians had a natural right to enter into military alliances with non-Christians to protect each other from harm, and he evoked the same sources and examples to prove his conclusion.[17]

In view of these similarities, the interpretation proposed by Borschberg, Van Ittersum and Tuck that *De societate* should be read alongside *De iure praedae* does indeed seem plausible. However, it should also be noted that

---

14 Tuck, 'Alliances with Infidels', pp. 74–76; Van Ittersum, *Profit and Principle*, p. 54.

15 This view was summarized in the early sixteenth century by Sylvestro Mazzolini da Prierio, also known by his Latin name as Sylvester Prierias, *Sylvestrinae Summae … pars prima* (Antverpiae: Ex officina Christophori Plantini, 1569), p. 93 (left column), on 'Bellum I' ('De bello publico'), 8, 3: 'Christiani habentes iustum bellum ad sui defensionem uti possunt (…) infidelibus pacificis non habentibus guerram activè aut passivè nobiscum imminente necessitate: aliter non' ('Christians having a just war for their own defense can use peaceful infidels who have no active or passive war with us; when necessity is pressing, not otherwise'). For other examples, see Tuck, 'Alliances with Infidels', pp. 64–66.

16 *IPC*, ed. Hamaker, p. 299, ed. Van Ittersum, p. 436.

17 For instance, in both *De iure praedae* and *De societate*, Grotius referred to the biblical examples of Abraham, Isaac, David and Solomon, who had entered into treaties of friendship and military alliances with 'infidel' rulers. Van Ittersum, *Profit and Principle*, p. 50.

De societate is a rather abstract treatise dealing with all kinds of partnerships between Christians and non-Christians, not only military alliances, but also, for instance, private associations, such as commercial contracts, marriages, and relations of servitude. Moreover, in his treatise, Grotius never explicitly refers to the East Indies or the VOC. Instead, he discusses examples of interreligious partnerships that are mentioned in the Bible and other sources (e.g., Roman and canon law). In this regard, *De societate* stands in sharp contrast to *De iure praedae*, in which Grotius explicitly defended the VOC's policies in the East Indies, focusing on particular alliances with non-Christian rulers such as the king of Johor.[18] Of course, the fact that Grotius does not mention the VOC's alliances in *De societate* does not mean that it is unrelated to the East-Indian context.[19] However, it does raise the question why Grotius refrained from discussing the VOC's alliances explicitly. As we will argue below, he probably intended to write a more general treatise on public and private partnerships between Christians and non-Christians, which pertained not only to the East-Indian context, but also to domestic debates about the legal position of non-Christians in the Dutch Republic. There are, for instance, important similarities—both in terms of content and use of sources—between *De societate* and the *Remonstrantie* of 1615, in which Grotius proposed a set of legal regulations for Jews residing in Holland and West-Friesland.

As our analysis of *De societate* will show, no sharp boundaries can be drawn between Grotius's views on partnerships with non-Christians in the international and domestic contexts. Indeed, as we will explain in this introduction, ideas about military alliances with non-Christians which Grotius developed in view of the East-Indian context were in fact closely related to his thoughts about legal partnerships with religious minorities living in Christian states and vice versa. For instance, the right to protect non-Christians from harm, which Grotius discussed in *De societate*, could simultaneously serve as an argument for overseas expansionism (e.g., protecting East-Indian nations from Portuguese aggression) *and* as a justification for religious toleration (e.g., protecting non-Christian minorities, who had fled from religious persecution and taken refuge in the Dutch Republic). In our view, Grotius's *De societate* should

18 On the VOC's alliance with the king of Johor see *IPC*, ed. Hamaker, pp. 297–299, ed. Van Ittersum, pp. 432–436.

19 For instance, in *De iure belli ac pacis*, Grotius also refrained from discussing the East Indies explicitly, yet scholars have convincingly demonstrated that, for instance, his theories about unequal treaties and monopoly contracts implicitly justified the VOC's policies. See Inge van Hulle, 'Grotius, Informal Empire and the Conclusion of Unequal Treaties', *Grotiana*, 37 (2016), 43–60 and Van Ittersum, 'The Long Goodbye', pp. 391–393.

thus be interpreted as a general treatise on legal partnerships between Christians and non-Christians that relates both to the VOC's policies of alliance-making in the East Indies *and* to debates about the rights of religious minorities in the Dutch Republic itself.[20] More specifically, we will argue that Grotius's treatise can be regarded as an important step in the development of his ideas about legal relations with non-Christians, starting with his early reflections in *De iure praedae* on alliances with non-Christian rulers in the East-Indian context, continuing with his proposal in the *Remonstrantie* for legal regulations for Jews in the Dutch Republic, and culminating in his general conclusions in *De iure belli ac pacis* regarding partnerships with 'strangers of the Christian religion' in both European and non-European contexts.

Before presenting Grotius's *De societate*, we would like to emphasize that our edition of the text should be considered a working document. This means that we did not intend to give definitive answers to all the questions raised by Grotius's manuscript and that further research will be necessary. In particular, we have not been able to solve all the reading problems in the manuscript. We have indicated possible alternative readings in notes to the transcription of the Latin text. Moreover, translating the text into English often required us to make interpretative choices, which are of course open to discussion. Hence, we invite other researchers to further improve our transcription and translation of the text, which is possible due to the availability of excellent, high resolution pictures of the manuscript itself on the website of Leiden University Library.[21] Moreover, in footnotes to the Latin text, we have focused on parallels with writings of Grotius in which he expressly discusses legal relations with non-Christians, such as *De iure praedae*, the *Remonstrantie*, and *De iure belli ac pacis*, but we have not systematically looked for parallels with his other writings. In particular, we have not compared the text of *De societate* with his later theological writings, even though this might be a promising field of research, as Grotius frequently discusses biblical examples in *De societate*. Moreover, we have not been able to identify all the sources to which Grotius refers in *De societate*. To mention the most intriguing example: in his reading notes on fol. 316 (2)^{v}, Grotius refers to 'c. 6 de Manubiis'. We suspect this might be a reference to chapter 6 of *De iure praedae*, although this cannot be determined with certainty.[22]

20 For this thesis, see also De Wilde, 'Hugo Grotius's *De societate*', pp. 1–18 (pp. 3–4).

21 https://digitalcollections.universiteitleiden.nl/view/item/936830#page/50/mode/1up.

22 In Latin, the words *manubiae* and *praeda* are closely related: *praeda* refers to the booty taken in war and *manubiae* to the money obtained from the sale of booty. As we explained above, the title *De iure praedae* was added to Grotius's manuscript by its nineteenth-century editor. Chapter 6 of *De iure praedae* deals with 'efficient causes of war'. One of

So, the analysis of Grotius's *De societate* we present in this introduction should not be seen as the end, but rather as the continuation of a scholarly debate about the text's meaning and significance. In particular, we hope that our edition of Grotius's text will stimulate new discussions about Grotius's views on legal partnerships with non-Christians, both in the international and domestic contexts.

2 History and Transmission of the Manuscript

The manuscript of *De societate* was originally part of a larger volume containing manuscripts and working papers of Grotius. The original folio numbers, written in Grotius's hand, are still visible at the top of the (uneven) pages. As Martine van Ittersum explains in a recent monograph, Grotius probably had his manuscripts bound in volumes when he was living in exile in Paris.[23] In May 1619, he had been convicted for high treason by a special court of the Estates General and sentenced to lifelong imprisonment at Loevestein Castle.[24] Following his arrest and conviction, his books and working papers were confiscated and removed from his house in Rotterdam.[25] In March 1621, Grotius

these efficient causes is the protection of the oppressed from injustice. At the beginning of the chapter, Grotius quotes Democritus in Latin: 'Injuria oppressos defendere pro viribus oportet et non negligere; illud enim justum bonumque est, hoc vero injustum et malum' (ed. Hamaker, p. 60, ed. Van Ittersum, p. 93: 'It behoves us to defend with all our might the victims of unjust oppression, and not to leave them neglected; for the former course is just and good, whereas the latter is unjust and wicked'). This quotation resembles the description Grotius gives in *De societate*: 'De defendendis oppressis v[ide] al[iter] c[aput] 6 de Manubiis' ('On the defense of the oppressed see otherwise c. 6 *de Manubiis*'). In *De iure praedae*, Grotius uses the words *manubiae* or *manubiis* several times (see, e.g., *IPC*, ed. Hamaker, pp. 54, 146 and 315). We thank Prof. em. Jan Hallebeek for helping us identifying this source.

23 Martine van Ittersum, *The Working Papers of Hugo Grotius: Transmission, Dispersal and Loss, 1604–1864* (Leiden: Brill, 2024), pp. 76–77 and 79. We thank Dr. Van Ittersum for generously sharing her manuscript.

24 The developments that led to Grotius's arrest, trial and imprisonment at Loevestein Castle are described in Henk Nellen, *Geen vredestichter is zonder tegensprekers: Hugo de Groot: Geleerde, staatsman, verguisd verzoener* (Amsterdam: Athenaeum, Polak & Van Gennep, 2021), pp. 91–101 and 109–131.

25 On the confiscation of Grotius's books and manuscripts: G. Moll, 'De confiscatie der goederen van Hugo de Groot', *Oud Holland*, 20 (2) (1902), 83–112, (pp. 83–102 and 107–112); P.C. Molhuysen, 'De bibliotheek van Hugo de Groot in 1618', *Medeelingen der Nederlandsche Akademie der Wetenschappen, nieuwe reeks, deel 6, afdeeling letterkunde*, 1–4 (1943), 45–49; Martine van Ittersum, 'Confiscated Books and Manuscripts: What Happened to the Personal Library and Archive of Hugo Grotius Following his Arrest on Charges of High

escaped from Loevestein, hidden in a bookchest. After his spectacular escape, he found a refuge in Paris. In the meantime, Grotius's wife Maria van Reigersberch lodged several unsuccessful appeals to the Court of Holland and Zeeland against the confiscation of her husband's possessions, until her request was partially granted in 1625 and then fully in 1630.[26] It would take several more years before Grotius finally received his books and working papers in Paris. By that time, he had become Swedish ambassador at the court of Louis XIII. According to Van Ittersum, Grotius probably sent his working papers to the binder in the late 1630s or early 1640s. Being an ambassador, he had both the means and need to systematically order his personal papers.[27]

It is unclear whether Grotius had the manuscript of *De societate* at his disposal when he wrote his magnum opus *De iure belli ac pacis* in the early 1620s in Paris. As we have seen, his possessions, including his manuscripts, had been confiscated in May 1619, and they were only partially returned to him after September 1625, when *De iure belli ac pacis* had already appeared in print. However, after his arrest in August 1618, Grotius's father Jan de Groot had managed to remove some manuscripts from his son's house in Rotterdam.[28] Moreover, in June 1619, his wife Maria obtained permission to remove thirty-one books, including 'two books written with the hand in folio', and send them to Loevestein.[29] It is, of course, possible that these included the manuscripts of *De iure praedae* and *De societate*. After his escape to Paris, Grotius repeatedly requested his family members to send his manuscripts to Paris. In the Spring of 1622, he specifically instructed his brother-in-law Nicolaes van Reigersberch to send him the manuscripts of his *Annales et historiae* (*Annals and Histories of the Dutch Revolt*) and his *Defensio capitis quinti maris liberi* (*Defense of the Fifth Chapter of Mare liberum*).[30] Moreover, in a letter of 20 June 1622, Grotius

---

Treason in August 1618?', in *Lost Books: Reconstructing the Print World of Pre-Industrial Europe*, ed. by Flavia Bruni and Andrew Pettegree (Leiden: Brill, 2016), pp. 362–385; Van Ittersum, *Working Papers*, pp. 127–160.

26 In 1625, the Court of Holland and Zeeland decided that half of the confiscated assets which Maria jointly owned with her husband had to be restored to her, and in 1630, the Court annulled the confiscation of all of Grotius's possessions. Van Ittersum, *Working Papers*, p. 157; Moll, 'De confiscatie der goederen van Hugo de Groot', pp. 98–99; Molhuysen, 'De bibliotheek van Hugo de Groot in 1618', p. 45.

27 Van Ittersum, *Working Papers*, p. 79.

28 Ibid., pp. 133–134.

29 After Grotius's escape, Maria received permission to leave Loevestein together with her maid and 'her belongings'. It is unclear whether she managed to take Grotius's books and manuscripts with her. Ibid., p. 143.

30 Letters from Grotius to Nicolaes van Reigersberch, 14 April and 10 June 1622, in BW, 2, p. 204 (no. 744) and p. 225 (no. 766).

thanked his brother Willem de Groot for sending him Vossius's copy of Stobaeus's *Eclogae physicae* as well as 'those childish works (*illis puerilibus*) of which we had great need'.[31] According to Peter Haggenmacher, the *puerilia* of the letter to Willem de Groot probably referred to the manuscript of *De iure praedae*.[32] It should be noted, however, that Grotius used the word *puerilia* in the plural: he probably referred to multiple manuscripts, and it is possible that these included both *De iure praedae* and *De societate*.[33] However, we cannot know for certain to which manuscripts Grotius referred in his letter, and hence, we simply do not know whether he had the manuscripts of *De societate* and *De iure praedae* at his desk when he wrote *De iure belli ac pacis*. We therefore agree with Van Ittersum that this can only be determined through a systematic comparison of the quotations and marginal references in these texts and in the 1625 and 1631 editions of *De iure belli ac pacis*.[34]

After Grotius's death in 1645, his manuscripts remained in the possession of his direct descendants for more than two centuries. When an inventory was made in 1778, it listed no less than 32 volumes of manuscripts and working papers (both of Grotius himself and his son Pieter), which were preserved in a 'big square white chest'.[35] As Van Ittersum explains, two volumes contained Grotius's papers on the East Indies as well as his early writings on natural law. Volume 18 contained documents relating to Grotius's advisory work for the Dutch East India Company: it consisted of reports, letters, petitions and other documents which Grotius had either received from or prepared for the

31 Letter from Grotius to Willem de Groot, 20 June 1622, in BW, 2, p. 225 (no. 767): 'Gratias ago pro transmisso Stobaei libro, item pro illis puerilibus quibus valde opus habebamus'.

32 According to the editor of Grotius's correspondence P.C. Molhuysen, the *puerilia* of the letter of 20 June 1622 referred to the *Annales et historiae* and *Defensio capitis*, which Grotius had specifically requested in his letters of 14 April and 10 June 1622 to his brother-in-law Nicolaes van Reigersberch. However, according to Haggenmacher, it is unlikely that Grotius, in his letter of 20 June, referred to his *Annales et historiae* and *Defensio capitis*, as it was addressed to his brother Willem, and not to his brother-in-law Nicolaes. Instead, Haggenmacher concludes that 'it is plausible that the *puerilia* of the letter to Willem refer in the first place to *De iure praedae*'. Peter Haggenmacher, *Grotius et la doctrine de la guerre juste* (Paris: Presses Universitaires de France, 1983), p. 386, n. 1871.

33 As Van Ittersum observes, it would have made sense for Willem de Groot to include the manuscript of *De iure praedae* in the shipment of Grotius's *puerilia*, if it was indeed in his possession. As we have seen, in his letters to Nicolaes van Reigersberch, Grotius had specifically requested his *Defensio capitis*, which was a reply to William Welwood's critique of *Mare liberum*. As chapter 12 of *De iure praedae* constituted the original text of *Mare liberum*, it would have been logical for Willem to assume that his brother also wished to receive *De iure praedae*. Van Ittersum, *Working Papers*, p. 158, n. 29.

34 Ibid., p. 157.

35 Ibid., pp. 565–572 (app. 1).

Company in the period between 1604 and 1615.[36] Volume 24 contained the manuscript of *De iure praedae*, along with other legal and political treatises from an early phase of his career, including the *Theses XI, Theses LVI, De pace* and *De societate publica cum infidelibus*.[37] The contents of this volume have been reconstructed by L.J. Noordhoff based on the original foliation: *De societate* was placed directly after a hand-written memorandum (not in Grotius's hand) on the legal grounds that could potentially be presented by the Spaniards for declaring the peace between the Northern Netherlands and the archdukes Albert and Isabella of Austria invalid (fol. 308–313)—a document that was probably written in 1607 or 1608.[38] Directly following *De societate* was a collection of reading notes and comments in Grotius's hand on Greek and Roman law, entitled *Ius Atticum et formulae et sententiae* (fol. 319–344).[39] Interestingly, the same volume also contained Grotius's *Remonstrantie* or draft regulations for Jews residing in Holland and West-Friesland of 1615 (fol. 1–34) as well as several other documents pertaining to the legal position of Jews in the Dutch Republic (fol. 198–211).[40]

---

36 Ibid., p. 369. These VOC papers are now preserved at the Dutch National Archives at the Hague, Collectie Hugo de Groot, supplement I, access 1.10.35.02, inv. 40.

37 Van Ittersum, *Working Papers*, p. 369. These manuscripts are now at the Leiden University Library, MS BPL 917 (*De iure praedae*) and MS BPL 922 I, fol. 276–286 (*Theses XI*), fol. 287–292 (*Theses LVI*), fol. 302–307 (*De Pace*) and fol. 314–318 (*De societate publica cum infidelibus*).

38 Grotius, *Observationes iuridicae contra pacem cum archiduce Alberto ineundam, non autographae*, Leiden University Library, MS BPL 922 Id, fol. 308–313. The manuscript contains some minor corrections in Grotius's hand. A transcription of the text has been published in W.J.M. van Eysinga, 'Eene onuitgegeven nota van De Groot', in *Sparsa collecta: Een aantal der verspreide geschriften van Jonkheer Mr. W.J.M. van Eysinga*, ed. by F.M. van Asbeck, E.N. van Kleffens, K.P. van der Mandele en J.R. Stellinga (Leiden: Sijthoff, 1958), pp. 488–504 (pp. 496–504); L.J. Noordhoff, *Beschrijving van het zich in Nederland bevindende en nog onbeschreven gedeelte der papieren afkomstig van Huig de Groot welke in 1864 zijn geveild* (Groningen: Noordhoff, 1953), p. 60.

39 Hugo Grotius, *Ius Atticum et formulae et sententiae*, Leiden University Library, MS BPL 922 II, fol. 319–344. Cf. Noordhoff, *Beschrijving*, p. 60.

40 Apart from the *Remonstrantie* itself (fol. 1–34), it contained an undated resolution of the states of Holland and West-Friesland concerning the legal order imposed on the Jews (fol. 198–200), copies of the decrees issued by Charles V against the 'new Christians' of 1549 and 1550 (fol. 205–211), and an anonymous response to the draft regulations on behalf of the Portuguese Jewish Community of Amsterdam (fol. 202–204). Today, these documents are preserved at the Ets Haim Library of the Portuguese synagogue in Amsterdam (MS EH 48 A 02 and MS EH 48 A 05) with the exception of the anonymous response, which is part of the Bibliotheca Rosenthaliana at the Amsterdam University Library (MS ROS 350/1).

In the second half of the nineteenth century, the collection of Grotius's manuscripts was still in the possession of his family. It was inherited by Hugo Cornets de Groot (1783–1864), a low-ranking tax collector from the village of Cuyck. After his death in 1864, Grotius's manuscripts were appropriated by his landlord, Jean-Baptiste Regouin, who used them to pay off his debts to Christian Snelleman, a tobacco merchant from Rotterdam. It was Snelleman who decided to offer the papers for sale at a public auction, organized by Martinus Nijhoff in The Hague.[41] Nijhoff hired the eminent bibliographer Pieter Anton Tiele to provide a description of the collection for the auction's catalogue. By that time, the volumes with Grotius's working papers were still in their original bindings. However, Nijhoff decided to have the manuscripts taken from their bindings, so that they could be offered as multiple lots (a strategy meant to increase the auction's profits).[42] At Nijhoff's request, Tiele disassembled several volumes and described their contents at document level.[43] In advance of the auction, Nijhoff reached out to potential buyers, offering a large collection of Grotius's manuscripts (that had originally been part of volume 24 in the inventory of 1778) to the University of Leiden. As Van Ittersum explains, the Law Faculty was particularly determined to acquire manuscripts that could raise Grotius's profile as a 'founder of modern international law'.[44] Due to a prior agreement with Nijhoff, it succeeded in buying the entire *collectanea juridica et politica* (lots 72–78) for 261 guilders. It contained the manuscript of *De iure praedae* (lot 72), the *Remonstrantie* and other documents relating to Jewish rights (lots 73–75), as well as a collection of about 450 pages of early legal and political treatises, including the manuscript of *De societate publica cum infidelibus* (lot 78).

3 Description of the Manuscript

The manuscript of *De societate* consists of six sheets, numbered fol. 314–317.[45] Two sheets are unnumbered. One of these was later inserted between folios 316 and 317; we will refer to it as fol. 316 (2). The other unnumbered sheet can

41 Van Ittersum, *Working Papers*, p. 417.

42 Ibid., p. 462.

43 Ibid., p. 486.

44 Ibid., p. 474.

45 Grotius, *De societate publica cum infidelibus*, Leiden University Library, MS Cod. BPL 922 Ie, fol. 314–318. https://digitalcollections.universiteitleiden.nl/view/item/936830#page/51/mode/1up.

be found at the end of the manuscript and has text only on the verso side; it will be referred to as fol. 318^{v}. The title of Grotius's treatise—*De societate publica cum infidelibus*—is mentioned twice, on fol. 314^{r} and on fol. 318^{v}. All in all, *De societate* consists of six pages of densely written text and another four pages with reading notes. All folio sheets are folded in the middle. The main text can be found on the right side of the page, with references to the sources on the left side. As Borschberg has pointed out, Grotius adopted the same working method in other manuscripts, for instance, in his *Theses LVI*, where he also wrote the main text on the right side of the page, leaving the left side open for additions and references to sources.[46] The main text of *De societate* consists of six pages and can be found on fol. 314, 315 and 317. Apart from the main text, there are four pages with reading notes, which can be found on fol. 316^{r}, 316 (2) and 318^{v}. The reading notes are written in two columns, on the left and right side of the page. On fol. 316 (2)^{v}, the notes are written first in two columns, then across the entire page, and then again in two columns.

Grotius inserted references to the sources he used in the main text, in marginal notes to the main text (on left side of the page) and in reading notes (on separate pages). Sometimes the same sources are mentioned at different places, allowing the reader to connect the main text to the reading notes. For instance, in the main text on fol. 314^{v}, Grotius presents his first conclusion that 'private and public persons' may enter into a 'pact' (*foedus*) with non-Christians with the aim not to harm one another. To support his conclusion, he refers to the biblical examples of the alliances of Abraham and Isaac with the Philistine king Abimelech, of Jacob with his father-in-law Laban, and of David and Solomon with Hiram, the king of Tyre, inserting references to the relevant passages in Genesis and Samuel.[47] These same examples are also mentioned in the reading notes on fol. 316 (1)^{r}, with short descriptions of their content. For instance, the alliance between Abraham and Abimelech is here characterized as an alliance 'of non-offensiveness and of cultivating friendship'.[48] However, not all the sources mentioned in the reading notes can be found in the main text, and conversely, not all sources cited in the main text reappear in the reading notes. For instance, in the main text on fol. 315^{r}, Grotius discusses several philosophical sources, including Cicero's

46 Borschberg, 'De societate', p. 357; Hugo Grotius, *Theses LVI*, Leiden University Library, MS Cod. BPL 922 ib, fol. 287–290.

47 Gen. 21.27; 26.29 and 31.49; 2 Sam. 5.11–12.

48 Grotius, *De societate*, fol. 316 (1)^{r}, left column.

De officiis and Seneca's *De beneficiis*, which are not mentioned in the reading notes. Conversely, the references to Alberico Gentili's *De iure belli* in the reading notes (fol. 316 (2)[v]) do not reappear in the main text. Hence, it is not always possible to relate the main text to the sources mentioned in the reading notes.

In our view, there are several reasons why *De societate* should probably be regarded as a draft. First of all, the manuscript is written in Grotius's own hand. There are several examples of manuscripts of Grotius of which we have clean copies in the hand of a clerk, sometimes with revisions made by Grotius himself.[49] However, in this case, no scribal copy has been preserved and we only have Grotius's autograph. Secondly, the content of *De societate* suggests that it was not a definitive version. It describes the skeleton structure of Grotius's argument, consisting of premises, propositions and conclusions. While the first three propositions are accompanied by lengthy explanations, later propositions and conclusions lack such explanations. This suggests that Grotius started writing out the text of *De societate*, but left it unfinished. A third reason for regarding the text of *De societate* as a draft is that often words or sentences have been crossed out or inserted. Moreover, the text contains some open variants, that is, alternative formulations about which Grotius still had to take a decision.[50] To give one significant example of a later insertion: in the title of the manuscript on fol. 314[r] the word *publica* is placed above the line. This suggests that the title was originally *De societate cum infidelibus*, 'On Partnership with Unbelievers', and that Grotius at a later stage added the word *publica* to the title: *De societate* publica *cum infidelibus*, thereby clarifying that the main focus of his treatise was on *public* partnership (e.g., treaties and alliances) between Christians and non-Christians. The reason for this shift of focus can perhaps be explained in light of the historical circumstances which led Grotius to write his treatise.

---

49 An example is the manuscript entitled *Observationes iuridicae contra pacem cum archiduce Alberto ineundam, non autographae*, pertaining to the peace negotiations with Spain, which was placed directly before *De societate* in volume 24 (Leiden University Library, MS BPL 922 Id, fol. 308–313). Another example is Grotius's *Remonstrantie* of 1615, which was written by a clerk with marginal additions in Grotius's hand (Ets Haim, MS EH 48 A 02). Grotius's letters to East-Indian rulers have been preserved both as drafts and as scribal copies with revisions made by Grotius himself. See, e.g., Dutch National Archives, Collectie Hugo de Groot, supplement I, access 1.10.35.02, inv. 40, fol. 344–345 (draft letter to the king of Ternate) and fol. 361–362 (copy of the letter to the king of Ternate, with marginal notes in Grotius's hand).

50 An example can be found on fol. 315[r], where Grotius writes 'his additamentis', adding the alternative formulation above the line: 'hoc additamento'.

4 Dating the Manuscript

As noted above, Borschberg believed *De societate* to be an early work of Grotius, which was written in the first decade of the seventeenth century.[51] The content and physical aspects of the manuscript, as well as the manner in which it has been transmitted, allow us to propose a more specific dating, viz. between 1606 and 1609. As we have seen, the manuscript of *De societate* was originally part of a volume (listed as volume 24 in the inventory of 1778) containing legal and political treatises from an early phase of Grotius's career. The most extensive treatise in this volume was *De iure praedae*, which was written between 1604 and 1606, and thoroughly revised in 1607 and 1608.[52] It was bound together with other manuscripts dating from the first decade of the seventeenth century. For instance, the manuscript relating to the peace negotiations between the Northern Netherlands and archdukes Albert and Isabella of Austria, which can be found directly before *De societate* in the volume (fol. 308–313), dated from 1607 or 1608.[53] Placed just before it was the manuscript of *De pace* (fol. 302–307), which probably originated from the same period and also related to the peace negotiations.[54] The volume also contained several other treatises from an early phase of Grotius's career. For instance, his *Commentarius in theses XI* (fol. 276–283) was probably written between 1603 and 1608,[55] while his *Theses LVI* (fol. 287–290) may have been produced a bit earlier, between 1602 and 1605.[56] However, the volume also included documents from the following decade, for instance, the *Remonstrantie* (fol. 1–34), which was written in, or shortly after, 1615.[57]

The sources to which Grotius refers in *De societate* allow us to propose a more precise dating of the manuscript. In the reading notes on fol. 318^{v}, Grotius

51 Borschberg, 'De societate', p. 356.

52 Martine van Ittersum, 'Dating the Manuscript of *De jure praedae* (1604–1608): What Watermarks, Foliation, and Quire Divisions Can Tell Us About Hugo Grotius's Development as a Natural Rights and Natural Law Theorist', *History of European Ideas*, 35 (2009), 125–193.

53 Noordhoff, *Beschrijving*, p. 60.

54 Peter Borschberg, 'De Pace: Ein unveröffentlichtes Fragment von Hugo Grotius über Krieg und Frieden', *Zeitschrift der Savigny-Stiftung für Rechtsgeschichte: Romanistische Abteilung*, 113 (1) (1996), 268–292 (p. 292).

55 Peter Borschberg, *Hugo Grotius' Commentarius in Theses XI: An Early Treatise on Sovereignty, the Just War, and the Legitimacy of the Dutch Revolt* (Bern: Peter Lang, 1994), p. 197.

56 Peter Borschberg, 'Grotius, the Social Contract, and Political Resistance: A Study of the Unpublished Theses LVI', *International Law and Justice Working Papers*, 7 (2006), 1–87.

57 Marc de Wilde, 'Offering Hospitality to Strangers: Hugo Grotius's Draft Regulations for the Jews', *Tijdschrift voor rechtsgeschiedenis*, 85 (2017), 391–433 (p. 404); Nellen, *Geen vredestichter*, pp. 101–106.

refers to a treatise on Mosaic law by Wilhelmus Zepperus. He gives a specific page number which corresponds to the relevant chapter in the 1604 edition of Zepperus's work.[58] However, the reference to Zepperus can be found on the last page of *De societate* (fol. 318^{v}) and it may have been added at a later stage, after Grotius had completed the main text. The text also contains two other references to an even later work, which may serve as a *terminus post quem* for dating the manuscript. In a marginal note to the main text on fol. 315^{v}, Grotius mentions Josephus Justus Scaliger's *Animadversiones in Eusebium*, of which the first edition appeared in 1606.[59] Grotius's reference to Scaliger's work is lapidary: no explanation is added. The work is mentioned in relation to Grotius's proposition that marriages between Christians and non-Christians should generally be condemned (since the main purpose of marriage is the education of children to the glory of God, which, according to Grotius, is 'not a little hindered' by such marriages).[60] A second reference to Scaliger's *Animadversiones* can be found on fol. 317^{r}, in a marginal note to Grotius's fifth conclusion that Christians and non-Christians can live together in one state.[61] It is of course possible that Grotius added these marginal references to Scaliger at a later stage, after completing the main text. No references to later works can be found in the manuscript. This means that Grotius probably wrote *De societate* in or after 1606.

Unfortunately, we have not been able to find a *terminus ante quem* for the manuscript of *De societate*. The text does not contain any references to historical events which make it possible to determine the latest date when it could have been written. However, there is another indication that we are dealing with a text that was probably written in, or not long after, 1606. The paper of fol. 316 (2) contains the watermark of a grape with a diamond shape cluster with a horn-shaped stem. This paper was produced by the papers mill of Troyes in France.[62] The same grape watermark can be found on a draft letter which

58 Wilhelmus Zepperus, *Legum mosaicarum forensium explanatio* (Herbornae Nassoviorum: Ex officina Christophori Corvini, 1604), IV.6 ('De federibus cum impiis et idololatris'), pp. 304–307.

59 See Josephus Justus Scaliger, *Thesaurus temporum* (Lugduni Batavorum: Excudebat Thomas Basson, 1606), with a separately paginated *Animadversiones in Chronologica Eusebii*. Grotius possessed a copy of Scaliger's book, which was confiscated after his arrest in 1618. See Molhuysen, 'De bibliotheek van Hugo de Groot in 1618', p. 51 (nr. 25).

60 Grotius, *De societate*, fol. 315^{v}, prop. 5.

61 Ibid., fol. 317^{r}, concl. 5.

62 Comparable grape watermarks have been found on documents from the period 1600–1650 in the Zeeland Archives. Th. and F. Laurentius, *Watermarks 1600–1650 Found in the Zeeland Archives* ('t Goy-Houten: Hes and De Graaf Publishers, 2007), pp. 34–36 and 238–242 (no. 553–574).

Grotius wrote on behalf of the Dutch East India Company to the king of Ternate.[63] This letter was probably written between the Summer and Winter of 1606.[64] The watermark can also be found on Grotius's draft of *De pace*, which, as we have seen, was written in the context of the peace and truce negotiations, between 1607 and 1609.[65] The fact that Grotius used the same paper for these manuscripts may serve as a rough indication that they were written around the same time. Of course, watermarks cannot give us any certainty with regard to the dating of manuscripts. It is, for instance, possible that Grotius used the same paper containing a particular watermark for several years. However, the paper containing the watermark of the diamond shape cluster was relatively inexpensive: Grotius seems to have used it only for drafts and reading notes.[66] It is, therefore, not very likely that he kept a stock of this inexpensive drafting paper for many years. This suggests that *De societate* was written either in 1606, or shortly after 1606, but not many years later.[67]

In the period between 1606 and 1609 (when a truce with Spain was concluded), Grotius had good reasons to be interested in the topic of *De societate*, and more specifically, in its main question if, and to what extent, it was permissible for Christians to enter into public partnerships with non-Christians. In 1606, the VOC directors had entrusted him with the task of writing a series of letters to Asian and East-Indian rulers to reconfirm their 'contracts of alliance' (*contracten van verbondt*).[68] In previous years, the VOC had

---

63 Hugo Grotius, Letter to the King of Ternate, Dutch National Archives, The Hague, Collectie Hugo de Groot, supplement I, access 1.10.35.02, inv. 40, fol. 344–345.

64 W.E. Smelt, 'Beschrijving eener verzameling papieren, afkomstig van Hugo de Groot', in *Inventarissen van Rijks- en andere archieven* (The Hague: Algemeene Landsdrukkerij, 1928), pp. 81–82 (at fol. 344–345) and Marc de Wilde, 'Allying with Unbelievers: Hugo Grotius's Letters to East-Indian Rulers', *Journal of the History of International Law*, 25 (1) (2023), 1–35 (p. 9).

65 Leiden University Library, MS BPL 922, fol. 302–307. The watermark of the grape with a diamond shape cluster can be found on fol. 302, 305 and 306. Borschberg, 'De Pace', p. 270.

66 For instance, in *De societate*, Grotius only used this paper for the reading notes on fol. 316 (2). By contrast, the main text was written on slightly larger and thicker paper, containing the watermarks of a crown and a crest (on fol. 314 and 317).

67 We thank Martine van Ittersum for her help in identifying the watermarks on *De societate* and for sharing her views on how they can be used to date Grotius's manuscripts. See also Van Ittersum, 'Dating the manuscript of *De iure praedae*', with a reference to the manuscripts in BPL 922 on p. 143.

68 These letters can be found at the Dutch National Archives, Collectie Hugo de Groot, supplement I, access 1.10.35.02, inv. 40, fol. 344–345 (draft letter to the king of Ternate), 359–360 (draft letter to the lords of Banda, with an instruction in Grotius's hand to send the same letter to the queen of Patani and the king of Bantam), 361–362 (copy of the letter to the king of Ternate, with marginal notes in Grotius's hand), 364 (draft letter to the

entered into alliances and treaties with a number of Asian and East-Indian rulers, including the 'emperor' of Malabar, the 'kings' of Johor, Tidore and Ternate, and the 'lords' of Ambon and the Banda islands.[69] In his letters to these rulers, Grotius defended the VOC's alliances: he claimed that the Dutch had united their trading companies, not only to better protect their own rights (e.g., to free navigation and trade), but also to 'liberate the princes and nations of the East Indies from the tyranny' of the Spaniards and Portuguese.[70] In his letters, Grotius reminded the East-Indian rulers of their obligations as allies of the Dutch, urging them to refrain from trading with other European nations. If the East-Indian rulers continued to deliver their spices to other nations, then the Dutch would no longer be able to finance the war fought on their behalf against the Iberian enemy.[71] Grotius's defense of the VOC's alliances with East-Indian rulers was, of course, not uncontroversial. A key question was whether alliances with non-Christian rulers could be legitimate if they were aimed against other Christians (such as the Spaniards and the Portuguese). As we will see, this would also be one of the main questions in *De societate publica cum infidelibus*.

In the winter of 1607–1608, negotiations started for a peace or truce agreement between the Dutch Republic and Spain. Grotius was asked by the VOC directors to work out a strategy for the Dutch negotiators, aimed at safeguarding the Company's strategic interests in Asia and the East Indies.[72] He prepared

lords of Ambon), 364v (draft letter to the king of Siam), 365–366 (copy of the letter to the king of Tidore, with marginal notes in Grotius's hand), 424 (draft letter to the king of Johor), 424–425 (draft letter to the emperor of Malabar), 430 (draft letter to the emperor of Borneo), and 430v (draft letter to the king of Tidore). An English translation of Grotius's letter to the king of Tidore has been published in Grotius, *Commentary on the Law of Prize and Booty*, ed. by Martine van Ittersum (Indianapolis: Liberty Fund, 2006), pp. 553–555 (app. 9). Borschberg has published transcriptions and English translations of the letters to the kings of Siam and Johor: Peter Borschberg, 'Cornelis Matelief, Hugo Grotius, and the King of Siam (1605–1616): Agency, Initiative and Diplomacy', *Modern Asian Studies*, 54 (1) (2020), 123–156 (p. 153–156, app. 2 and 3 (transcriptions) and 139–140 (translations)). The other letters are discussed in De Wilde, 'Allying with Unbelievers: Hugo Grotius's Letters to East-Indian Rulers'.

69 F.W. Stapel, 'Corpus diplomaticum Neerlando-Indicum: Verzameling van politieke contracten en verdere verdragen door de Nederlanders in het Oosten gesloten, van privilegebrieven aan hen verleend, etc'. *Bijdragen tot de taal-, land- en volkenkunde van Nederlands Indië*, 57 (1907), 30–48 (XIII–XX).

70 Dutch National Archives, The Hague, Collectie Hugo de Groot, supplement I, access 1.10.35.02, inv. 40, fol. 344r (Ternate), 359r (Banda) and 365r (Tidore).

71 Ibid., fol. 344v and 362r (Ternate), 359v (Banda), 366r and 430v (Tidore). See De Wilde, 'Allying with Unbelievers'.

72 On Grotius's involvement in the peace negotiations of 1607 and 1608: Van Ittersum, *Profit and Principle*, pp. 189–282 and Borschberg, 'Hugo Grotius and the East Indies', p. 70.

two drafts of a memorandum, in which he sketched three possible scenarios: under the first scenario, both parties would be free to trade in the East Indies and hostilities would cease. According to the second, the Dutch would agree to withdraw from the East Indies and the VOC would end its activities there in a few years. The third scenario was that notwithstanding the peace in Europe, the war in the East Indies would be continued.[73] As Grotius suggested, the first scenario was the preferred outcome, but if it would not be accepted, then the Dutch negotiators should seek to achieve the more realistic third scenario: a treaty permitting a continuation of the war beyond the Line (i.e., the tropical Line of Cancer). In his memorandum, Grotius expressly referred to the VOC's 'correspondence, friendships and alliances' with East-Indian rulers.[74] As Grotius explained, the Company had entered into these alliances on behalf of the Dutch Estates General, and these rulers could not be left to the mercy of the Spaniards and Portuguese without seriously damaging the Dutch reputation.[75] In February 1608, the VOC directors enthusiastically approved Grotius's memorandum and the Estates General adopted it as its official negotiating position.[76] In accordance with Grotius's proposal the Dutch and Spanish rights in the East Indies would be determined on the basis of the legal principle of *uti possidetis*: parties would continue to possess those territories they already possessed at the moment the truce would come into effect.[77] In April 1608, the VOC directors therefore sent instructions to their officials overseas to enter into as many treaties and alliances with East-Indian rulers as possible before the truce would take effect.[78]

It is not unlikely that Grotius wrote *De societate* between 1606 and 1609. In these years, the issue of the legitimacy of alliances with non-Christian rulers in Asia and the East Indies was particularly high on the agenda of both Grotius and the VOC directors. Grotius's thesis in *De societate* that both 'private and public persons' were permitted to enter into alliances with non-Christians with

73 Hugo Grotius, 'Vertoog opgemaakt voor de Oost Indië Compagnie betreffende de houding, door deze bij de onderhandelingen met Spanje aan te nemen' (undated), Dutch National Archives, The Hague, Collectie Hugo de Groot, supplement 1, access 1.10.35.02, inv. 40, fol. 295–299 (first version) and 405–413 (second version), at fol. 406^r. On Grotius's memorandum: Van Ittersum, *Profit and Principle*, pp. 191–192 and 227–244; Borschberg, 'Hugo Grotius and the East Indies', pp. 71–72.

74 Grotius, 'Vertoog', fol. 405^v.

75 Ibid., fol. 405^v.

76 Van Ittersum, *Profit and Principle*, p. 192.

77 Ibid., p. 265; Grotius, 'Vertoog', fol. 406^r.

78 Van Ittersum, *Profit and Principle*, p. 265 and Borschberg, 'Hugo Grotius and the East Indies', pp. 71–72.

the aim of protecting each other from harm[79] could thus serve as a justification for the VOC's policy of allying with East-Indian rulers against the Spaniards and Portuguese. It is true that Grotius had already defended the VOC's alliances as early as 1604, when he had argued in *De iure praedae* that the Company was waging a 'public war' against the Portuguese on behalf of its non-Christian ally, the Sultan of Johor.[80] But as we have seen, the references to Scaliger's *Animadversiones* suggest that Grotius wrote *De societate* somewhat later, that is, in or shortly after 1606. By that time, Grotius had become personally involved in building the VOC's network of alliances in the East Indies. Perhaps Grotius's letters to East-Indian rulers prompted him to write *De societate* to develop his ideas about interreligious alliances in a more systematic manner: the main question was no longer whether these alliances were permissible at all, but rather under what legal conditions they were justified. The treatise may also have been written in conjunction with the diplomatic initiative of April 1608, and the Company's policy to conclude as many treaties and alliances with East-Indian rulers as possible before the truce with Spain would take effect. Although it remains uncertain, the combination of factors—references to particular sources, the diamond shape grape watermark, the historical context of the peace and truce negotiations—all point to a dating between 1606 and 1609.

5 Explaining the Title

Before analyzing the content of Grotius's treatise, we should first consider its title: *De societate publica cum infidelibus*. Borschberg translates it as 'Of Public Society with Non-Christians'.[81] Other scholars have left the Latin title untranslated.[82] The word *societas* is particularly difficult to translate. In Grotius's time, *societas* did not have the same connotations it has today, of a community of people sharing the same laws and customs. Instead, for Grotius, *societas* also referred to relations between communities (e.g., 'nations' or religious communities), which often had their own customs and laws, while also sharing certain laws (e.g., those of natural law and the *ius gentium*). The legal term *societas* originated from Roman private law: it was one of the consensual contracts, whereby two or more persons agreed to co-operate for a common purpose (often a busi-

79 Grotius, *De societate*, fol. 314^v.

80 *IPC*, ed. Hamaker, p. 297, ed. Van Ittersum, pp. 432–433.

81 Borschberg, *Hugo Grotius, the Portuguese and Free Trade*, p. 56.

82 See, e.g., Tuck, 'Alliances with Infidels', p. 75 and Condorelli, 'Grotius's Doctrine of Alliances with Infidels', p. 30; Van Ittersum, *Profit and Principle*, p. 49.

ness association).[83] The more specific term *societas publica* was unknown to Roman law: what came closest was *societas publicanorum*, an association of tax collectors.[84] It was Cicero who first used the private law concept of *societas* as a model for understanding *public* associations. Thus, in *De re publica*, he defined the state (*res publica*) as 'an assemblage of people in large numbers associated [*sociatus*] in an agreement with respect to justice and a partnership for the common good'.[85] Building on Roman law and Cicero, medieval jurists and theologians developed the concept of *societas publica*. For instance, in his *Liber contra impugnantes Dei cultum et religionem* (ca. 1256), Thomas Aquinas distinguished between a *societas privata*, an association for private purposes (e.g., a business association), and a *societas publica*, which was created when men assembled to establish a state.[86]

Like Cicero and Aquinas, Grotius used the term *societas publica* to define the state (*res publica*): he concluded that 'the highest public partnership is the union of the state (*summa publica societas est unio reipublicae*)'.[87] However, he also employed the term *societas publica* to refer to treaties and alliances *between* states, using the words *societas* and *foedus* as synonyms.[88] As we have seen, in *De societate*, he discussed not only 'public societies', but also 'private societies', such as commercial contracts, marriages, and relations of servitude (e.g., relations between masters and slaves or servants). On the first page of his treatise, he explicitly referred to Aquinas's distinction between *societas privata* and *societas publica*, that is, between private and public societies.[89] However, he also explained that 'in both cases the principle [was] almost the same [*in*

83 For a textbook discussion of *societas* in Roman private law: Barry Nicholas, *An Introduction to Roman Law* (Oxford: Clarendon, 1977), pp. 185–187. On the historical development of *societas*: Max Kaser, *Das römische Privatrecht* (Munich: Beck, 1975), vol. 2, pp. 409–415.

84 Wolfgang Kunkel, *Roman Legal and Constitutional History*, trans. by J.M. Kelly (Oxford: Oxford University Press, 1966), p. 40.

85 Cicero, *De re publica*, trans. by Clinton Walker Keyes (Cambridge, MA; Harvard University Press), 1.25.39: 'coetus multitudinis iuris consensu et utilitatis communione sociatus'. On Cicero's definition of the state as societas, see Elizabeth Asmis, 'The State as Partnership: Cicero's Definition of Res Publica in his Work on the State', *History of Political Thought*, 25 (2004), 569–599.

86 Aquinas, *Liber contra impugnantes Dei cultum et religionem*, pars 2, c. 2, corp. On Aquinas's distinction between *societas privata* and *societas publica*: Nicholas Aroney, 'Subsidiarity, Federalism, and the Best Constitution, Thomas Aquinas on City, Province and Empire', *Law and Philosophy*, 26 (2) (2007), 161–228 (p. 186). Cf. De Wilde, 'Hugo Grotius's *De societate*', pp. 424–425, n. 11.

87 Grotius, *De societate*, fol. 317^r.

88 See, e.g., ibid., fol. 314^v, concl. 1 (and *exempla*).

89 Grotius, *De societate*, fol. 314^r, prem. 8 and fol. 315^v, prop. 3, sub lim. 3.

utroque ferme eadem est ratio]'.[90] For Grotius, the distinction between 'public' and 'private' was not absolute,[91] so that, for instance, public alliances with non-Christians could be concluded by private actors (e.g., the VOC as a private trading company) on behalf of a public authority (e.g., the Dutch Estates General).[92] As Grotius explained in *De societate*, 'public societies' were governed by 'almost the same' principle as 'private societies:' for instance, alliances between states and contracts between private parties were in general permissible, provided that they did not undermine the unity of the state or the Christian religion.

As other scholars have pointed out, the concept of *societas* would take center stage in Grotius's later work.[93] Thus, in *De iure belli ac pacis* (1625), Grotius famously defined human nature itself in terms of an 'impelling desire for society [*appetitus societatis*]', which he later identified with the Stoic doctrine of 'sociability [*οἰκείωσις*]'.[94] He explained that man's 'desire for society' was to be understood in a Stoic sense as a 'certain inclination [of man] to live with those of his own kind, not in any manner whatever, but peaceably, and in a community regulated according to the best of his understanding'.[95] From this 'maintenance of social order [*societatis custodia*]', to which man was by nature inclined, the main principles of the 'law properly so called', that is, natural law, could be rationally deduced. These included the principle that one should abstain from taking away someone else's property, that one should restore what belonged to another (including the profit one had received from it), that one should fulfill one's promises, that one should compensate for the losses

90 Ibid., fol. 315r.

91 This has also been noted by other Grotius scholars. For instance, Benjamin Straumann has demonstrated that Grotius modelled the titles for *public* war after legal remedies from Roman *private* law. Benjamin Straumann, 'Is Modern Liberty Ancient? Roman Remedies and Natural Rights in Hugo Grotius's Early Works on Natural Law', *Law and History Review*, 27 (1) (2009), 55–86. See also Benjamin Straumann, *Roman Law in the State of Nature: The Classical Foundations of Hugo Grotius's Natural Law* (Cambridge: Cambridge University Press, 2019).

92 See also *IPC*, ed. Hamaker, pp. 298–299, ed. Van Ittersum, p. 434, where Grotius uses the term *societas* to refer to the alliance with the Sultan of Johor, which had been concluded by the VOC on behalf of the Dutch Estates General. In this context, the term *societas* is translated by Gwladys Williams as 'alliance' (or 'alliances' in the plural).

93 See, *inter alia*, Laurens Winkel, 'Les origines antiques de l'appetitus societatis de Grotius', *Tijdschrift voor rechtsgeschiedenis*, 68 (2000), 393–403; Benjamin Straumann, 'Oikeiosis and appetitus societatis: Hugo Grotius' Ciceronian Argument for Natural Law and Just War', *Grotiana*, 24–25 (2003), 41–66 and Hans Blom, 'Sociability and Hugo Grotius', *History of European Ideas*, 41 (2015), 589–604.

94 *IBP*, prol. 6 (the reference to the Stoic *οἰκείωσις* was added in the edition of 1631).

95 *IBP*, prol. 6 (trans. Kelsey).

incurred by one's fault, and that one should inflict punishment on others if deserved.[96] For Grotius, these fundamental principles of natural law served as the foundation not only of *private* law (e.g., the law of property, contracts and torts), but also of *public* law (e.g., constitutional law, criminal law and public international law). In *De societate*, Grotius first developed the term *societas* as a general legal concept underlying private and public partnerships with non-Christians: in *De iure belli ac pacis*, it came to be identified as the main source of natural law itself.

Just as complex as Grotius's use of the term *societas publica* was his use of the term *infideles*. Who were the 'infidels' to whom Grotius refers in the title of his treatise? As we have seen, Borschberg translates *De societate publica cum infidelibus* as 'Of Public Society with Non-Christians'. He thereby suggests that it primarily refers to non-Christians, that is, to those who do not believe in Christ or Christian doctrine. However, as Borschberg himself notes, Grotius not only discusses partnerships with non-Christians, but also with 'heretics [*haeretici*]'. Indeed, throughout the text, he uses the standard expression 'societas cum infidelibus aut haereticis [*society with infidels or heretics*]', suggesting that non-Christians and heretics belong to the same general category of non-believers.[97] As Grotius specifies, there are two kinds of 'infidels', namely 'those who never belonged to the Church', and 'those who departed from it, or are expelled by an ecclesiastical judgement'.[98] We may assume that the first category includes Jews, Muslims and 'pagans'.[99] Grotius may have thought of the Muslim populations of the East Indies as well as non-Christian minorities (e.g., Jews) in the Dutch Republic itself. The second category relates to heretics and apostates: it is uncertain whom Grotius has in mind, as he does not give specific examples. From the perspective of some of the Catholic (and Counter-Reformatory) sources he uses in *De societate* (e.g., Sylvester, Cajetanus and Vitoria), Dutch Protestants could, of course, themselves be regarded as heretics. In the context of the peace negotiations with Spain, Grotius's aim may have been to convince international audiences that a peace treaty with the Dutch was binding, even if the Spaniards regarded them as heretics.[100] Interestingly, elsewhere in *De soci-*

96 *IBP*, prol. 8.

97 See, *inter alia*, Grotius, *De societate*, fol. 314ᵛ, introd., 314ᵛ, prop. 1 and concl. 1, prop. 2 et ampl., 315ᵛ, prop. 3 and lim. 3.

98 Ibid., fol. 315ᵛ, in prop. 3.

99 Cf. Hugo Grotius, *De veritate religionis christianae* (Lugduni Batavorum: Ex officina Ioannis Maire, 1629 [1627]), IV (p. 134): 'singula religionum genera, quae se Christianis opponent, Paganismus puta, Iudaismus & Mahumetismus'.

100 In the memorandum which Grotius prepared for the peace negotiations with Spain (which was placed directly before *De societate* in BPL 922), he referred to some of the

etate, Grotius refers to a third category, of those who 'wish to be considered as faithful [*ii qui Fideles haberi velint*]', which should probably be read as a pejorative reference to Catholics (e.g., the Spaniards and Portuguese).[101]

Grotius's understanding of these distinctions seems to have been informed by Aquinas's *Summa theologiae*, which is cited on the first page of *De societate*.[102] Aquinas had distinguished between three types of unbelief. First, there were the 'pagans or heathens [*pagani sive gentiles*]', that is, those who had never heard the Gospel. Second, there were the 'Jews [*Iudaei*]', who had heard the message of Christ, but did not believe that he was the redeemer. The third category consisted of 'heretics [*haeretici*]', who had accepted that Christ was the redeemer, but distorted his message.[103] Addressing the question whether 'the unbelief of pagans or heathens [was] graver than other kinds', Aquinas emphasized the importance of free will in accepting or rejecting the message of Christ.[104] Those who had intentionally rejected the message of Christ sinned more grievously than those who had never heard it, while those who had accepted his message, but then distorted it, sinned more grievously than those who had not accepted it.[105] Aquinas concluded that 'the unbelief of heretics, who confess their belief in the Gospel, and resist that faith by corrupting it, is a more grievous sin than that of the Jews, who have never accepted the Gospel faith. Since, however, they accepted the figure of that faith in the Old

same Catholic sources he used in *De societate*, including Panormitanus and Sylvester. The aim of Grotius's memorandum was to determine on what legal grounds a peace treaty with Spain could potentially be declared null and void. Among the legal grounds that could be invoked to invalidate the treaty, Grotius mentioned the decree of the Council of Constance (1414–1418), according to which promises made to heretics were not binding, adding that 'there is little doubt that the King of Spain regards us as heretics' (fol. 309r). He also explained that, under canon law, public acts of those who were excommunicated were considered invalid. He even suggested that the pope could give away as booty the lands and possessions of heretics and the excommunicated to whomever he desired. As proof Grotius referred to Sylvester's commentary on *excommunicatio* and Panormitanus's gloss on c. *quod super de voto*—a source he also invoked in *De societate* (fol. 316 (2)v, left column). See Grotius, *Observationes iuridicae contra pacem cum archiduce Alberto ineundam, non autographae*, BPL 922 Id, fol. 308–313 (with references to Sylvester on fol. 309r and Panormitanus on fol. 308r and 309v); Van Eysinga, 'Eene onuitgegeven nota van De Groot', pp. 488–504 (pp. 498–499).

101 Grotius, *De societate*, fol. 317r, concl. 3. See De Wilde, 'Hugo Grotius's *De societate*', pp. 429–430.

102 Grotius, *De societate*, fol. 314r, prem. 1. The reference is to *S. Th.* 2a 2ae, q. 10, a. 10. Borschberg, 'De societate', p. 360.

103 *S. Th.* 2a 2ae, q. 10, a. 5, resp. Borschberg, 'De societate', p. 360.

104 Cf. Borschberg, 'De societate', p. 360.

105 *S. Th.* 2a 2ae, q. 10, a. 6, resp.

Law, which they corrupt by their false interpretations, their unbelief is a more grievous sin than that of the heathens, because the latter have not accepted the Gospel faith in any way at all'.[106] In other words, according to Aquinas, the sins of the pagans or heathens, who had never heard the Gospel, were less grievous than those of the Jews, who had heard the Gospel but rejected it, while the sins of the Jews were less grievous than those of the heretics, who had distorted the message of Christ. As Aquinas concluded, 'speaking absolutely, the unbelief of heretics [was] the worst'.[107]

In *De societate*, Grotius seems to share Aquinas's conclusion that the unbelief of heretics is worse than that of pagans and Jews. While Christians are generally allowed to live together with pagans and Jews, Grotius warns that they 'must abstain from intimate relations and social intercourse with those who have fallen from the Church, or have been condemned by its judgement: because this is so arranged for a special reason, that they should return to shame and repentance'.[108] However, instead of Aquinas's threefold distinction between 'pagans', 'Jews' and 'heretics', Grotius presents a twofold distinction between 'those who never belonged to the Church' (i.e., non-Christians) and 'those who departed from it, or are expelled by an ecclesiastical judgement' (i.e., heretics or apostates).[109] Crucially, in Grotius's twofold distinction, the Jews no longer constitute a separate category, but they are now grouped together with other non-Christians, including those who have never heard the Gospel (Aquinas's 'pagans or heathens'). By placing 'Jews' and 'pagans' in the same category of 'those who never belonged to the Church', Grotius implicitly introduces a more positive understanding of the Jews: like pagans who have never heard the message of Christ, the Jews may not be punished for their ignorance. Indeed, in some respects, the Jews seem to be placed *above* other non-Christians. This is the consequence of Grotius's focus on examples from the Old Testament, in which the Jews appear as God's chosen people and as an example for the believers. Grotius would further develop these more positive views of the Jews in his *Remonstrantie*, where he observed that '[t]he pagans have

106 *S. Th.* 2a 2ae, q. 10, a. 6, resp.: 'infidelitas haereticorum, qui profitentur fidem Evangelii, et ei renituntur eam corrumpentes, gravius est peccatum quam Iudaeorum, qui fidem Evangelii numquam susceperunt. Sed quia susceperunt eius figuram in veteri lege, quam male interpretantes corrumpunt: ideo etiam eorum infidelitas est gravius peccatum quam infidelitas gentilium, qui nullo modo fidem Evangelii susceperunt'. English translation: *The Summa Theologiae of St. Thomas Aquinas*, trans. Fathers of the English Dominican Province (Lawrence Shapcote) (London: Burns, Oates and Washbourne, ca. 1916).

107 *S. Th.* 2 2ae, q. 10, a. 6, concl.: 'infidelitas haereticorum est pessima'.

108 Grotius, *De societate*, fol. 315^{v}, lim. to prop. 3.

109 Ibid., fol. 315^{v}, in prop. 3.

false Gods. The Mohammedans have a false Prophet. The Jews at any rate have the true God and the true Prophets'.[110]

6 Structure of the Text

De Societate begins with a short introduction, in which Grotius presents his main question: 'if and to what degree it be allowed to Christians to enter into a partnership with non-believers, or even heretics'.[111] As Grotius explains, this question is old, yet still frequently discussed in his own time. The sources to which Grotius refers in the main text and reading notes indicate that the question is indeed very old: they include Scripture, Roman law (e.g., the Codex Theodosianus), medieval theology and canon law (e.g., Gratian, Aquinas, Panormitanus, and Oldradus) as well as the later scholastic tradition (e.g., Cajetanus, Sylvester, and Vitoria). Grotius also refers to legal and theological sources from his own time (e.g., Gentili, Zepperus and Scaliger), albeit less frequently. In the introduction of *De societate*, he observes that in these sources, the question if and to what degree public partnerships with non-believers are allowed has been considered primarily on the basis of *exempla*, while the underlying principles or reasons for particular solutions have been insufficiently explained. It is true that many of the sources mentioned in *De societate* (in particular, medieval scholastic sources) are casuistic, in the sense that concrete cases and examples are discussed to justify particular solutions: examples of 'societies' with non-believers are thus discussed in glosses or commentaries on questions pertaining, for instance, to 'unbelief', 'war', 'charity', or 'marriage'.[112] Unlike his predecessors, Grotius wants to address the question regarding the permissibility of 'public societies' with non-believers in a more comprehensive and systematic (i.e., syllogistic) manner.

Apart from the brief introduction, the text of *De societate* consists of ten premises, nine propositions and nine conclusions. Grotius suggests that the propositions are rationally deduced from the premises and that the conclusions follow logically from the premises and propositions. For instance, after presenting his first proposition, he adds the words: 'ex primo praemisso', implying that this proposition derives 'from the first premise'.[113] He then continues

110 Grotius, *Remonstrantie*, fol. 7^{r}, p. 83, trans., p. 203.

111 Grotius, *De societate*, fol. 314^{r}, introd.

112 See, e.g., *S. Th.* 2a 2ae, q. 10: 'De infidelitate'; Sylvester Prierias, *Sylvestrinae Summae*, pp. 89–98: 'De bello'.

113 Grotius, *De societate*, fol. 314^{v}, prop. 1; cf. fol. 314^{r}, prem. 1.

with a brief explanation, before adding the words '[u]nde sequitur conclusio', indicating that the conclusion follows from his first proposition.[114] According to the first proposition, Christians have a duty to refrain from harming non-believers and heretics. As Grotius explains, this proposition follows from the first premise that an 'error of faith' does not change the obligations that originate from the law of nature. The proposition then leads to the first conclusion that 'it is permissible for both private and public persons to enter into a pact with non-believers or heretics not to harm one another'.[115] According to Grotius, this conclusion follows logically and thus necessarily from his first premise and proposition. However, the relationship between premises, propositions and conclusions is not always as straightforward and logical as in the discussed example. Often conclusions are not placed directly after the relevant propositions,[116] and sometimes they even precede them.[117] Moreover, it is not always certain from which premises particular propositions are derived, as the relevant premises are not always indicated by Grotius. For this reason, the intricate system of premises, propositions and conclusions remains difficult to decipher.

The premises Grotius presents in *De societate* are in general relatively short; in most cases, they consist of a single sentence. Sometimes, they contain distinctions that are relevant for analyzing the main question (e.g., between those who belong to the church and those who do not), which are further developed in the propositions and conclusions.[118] Premises 7 to 10 are particularly short; they seem to be hastily added and contain distinctions relating to the different types of infidels and partnerships. By contrast, the propositions and conclusions tend to be more extensive: they are followed by (sometimes lengthy) explanations, in which relevant examples and sources are discussed. Moreover, Grotius often adds 'limitations' or 'amplifications' to his propositions and conclusions, which are indicated with the abbreviations 'lim[itatio]' and 'ampl[ificatio]' and separately numbered. For instance, his second proposition is followed by one amplification and two limitations. As Grotius indicates, these limitations and amplifications follow from the premises.[119] Often a particular

114 Ibid., fol. 314^r, prem. 1.

115 Ibid., fol. 314^v, concl. 1; cf. fol. 314^r, prem. 1.

116 For instance, the second conclusion is placed after the fifth proposition, to which it seems unrelated. Ibid., fol. 317^r, concl. 2.

117 For instance, the seventh conclusion is placed before the seventh proposition. Ibid., fol. 317^v, concl. 7.

118 Ibid., fol. 314^r, prem. 7 and 8. The distinction between those who belong to the church and those who do not is further developed in the explanation to prop. 3 on fol. 315^v.

119 See, for instance, fol. 315^r, prop. 2, lim. 2: 'ex 2 P[raemissio]ne'.

proposition is developed on the basis of one premise and then limited on the basis of another. An example is the second proposition, according to which the faithful are allowed to do good to non-believers.[120] This proposition is first amplified on the basis of the first premise, in the sense that depending on the circumstances, it is not only allowed (i.e., a right), but also necessary (i.e., a duty) to do good to non-believers.[121] The proposition is then limited on the basis of the second premise, in that preference should be given to the faithful over non-believers and heretics, and that no harm may be brought to the Christian religion.[122]

The system of premises, propositions and conclusions of *De societate* is in some respects comparable to the axiomatic-deductive system which Grotius first used in *De iure praedae* and further developed in *De iure belli ac pacis*.[123] As Grotius explained in the prolegomena of *De iure praedae*, just as mathematicians usually begin their demonstrations by presenting certain axioms on which all persons can easily agree, jurists should preferably begin by outlining certain laws and rules of the most general nature, which no rational person can disagree with.[124] From these general laws, the main conclusions can be rationally deduced. In his prolegomena, Grotius presents a framework consisting of nine rules and thirteen laws, from which he derives his conclusions. One of these laws is the so-called law of non-offensiveness: 'let no one inflict injury upon his fellow'.[125] This law reappears in the form of a proposition

---

120 Ibid., fol. 314^{v}, prop. 2.

121 Ibid., fol. 314^{v}, prop. 2, ampl.

122 Ibid., fol. 315^{r}, prop. 2, lim. 1 and 2. The structure of the text is not entirely clear due to changes made by Grotius himself. What was originally the second limitation to the second proposition—that 'greater friendship and familiarity should be cultivated with the faithful than with the non-believers'—was later renumbered as the first limitation to the third proposition that '[i]t is permissible to have some friendship and familiarity with non-believers and with heretics' (ibid., fol. 315^{r}, prop. 3, lim. 1 and fol. 315^{v}, prop. 3). Grotius did not cross out the original numbering in the main text, while adding the new numbering in the margins. The first limitation to the second proposition was divided into two parts (renumbered as 'I. limit. [1]' and 'II. lim.'), while the second limitation to the second proposition was renumbered as the first limitation to the third proposition ('I. lim. III. prop. [2]'; the original numbering is placed between brackets). These changes perhaps explain why he first discusses the limitations to his third proposition (on fol. 315^{r-v}) before presenting the proposition itself (on fol. 315^{v}).

123 For the use and development of the axiomatic-deductive system in Grotius, see: Laurens Winkel, 'Problems of Legal Systematization from *De iure praedae* to *De iure belli ac pacis*', *Grotiana*, 26–28 (2005–2007), 61–78.

124 *IPC*, ed. Hamaker, p. 7, ed. Van Ittersum, p. 17.

125 *IPC*, ed. Hamaker, p. 13, ed. Van Ittersum, p. 27 (law 3).

in *De societate*, where it is applied to non-Christians and heretics: 'To refrain from harming non-believers and heretics in general is not only permissible for Christians, but also necessary'.[126] Another law presented in *De iure praedae* is the law of (individual and collective) protection: 'Individual citizens should not only refrain from injuring other citizens, but should furthermore protect them, both as a whole and as individuals'.[127] This law seems to be related to the amplification of the second proposition of *De societate*, according to which Christians should not only refrain from harming non-Christians, but should also provide assistance to them, especially when they ask for help.[128] In both *De iure praedae* and *De societate*, these laws and propositions then serve to support the conclusion that it is permissible for Christians to enter into alliances with non-Christians to protect each other from harm.[129] According to Grotius's axiomatic-deductive system, this conclusion follows logically, and thus necessarily, from the premises and propositions. However, as our analysis of the main text of *De societate* will show, the relations between premises, propositions and conclusions are not always as logical and necessary as Grotius's axiomatic-deductive system suggests.

7 Analysis of the Text

7.1 *The Ten Premises*

Addressing the question 'if and to what degree it be allowed to Christians to enter into a partnership with non-believers, or even heretics', Grotius begins by presenting ten premises, from which his propositions and conclusions are derived. According to his first premise, a distinction should be made between two types of 'societies:' on the one hand, the community between men that originates from nature, which is governed by primary and secondary natural law, and, on the other, the ecclesiastical community, which is governed by divine law and the law of the church. The concepts of 'primary' and 'secondary natural law' had been developed by medieval jurists and theologians on the basis of Roman law: while primary natural law governed relations between all living (i.e., human and non-human) beings, secondary natural law applied only to human beings endowed with reason.[130] Grotius had first used these concepts

126 Grotius, *De societate*, fol. 314^{v}, prop. 1.

127 *IPC*, ed. Hamaker, p. 21, ed. Van Ittersum, p. 37 (law 7).

128 Grotius, *De societate*, fol. 314^{v}, prop. 2.

129 Ibid., concl. 3; *IPC*, ed. Hamaker, p. 298, ed. Van Ittersum, p. 434.

130 *Dig.* 1.1.1.3–4 (Ulpian); on the genesis of the concepts of primary and secondary natural law

in *De iure praedae*, in which he identified secondary natural law with the primary law of nations, that is, the body of legal norms that followed from natural reason and that applied to all nations.[131] In the first premise of *De societate*, Grotius explains that an 'error of faith' (*error in fide*) does not change 'those things that pertain to natural law and the protection of [the] universal community [of mankind]'.[132] In this context, he refers to Aquinas, who had argued that 'divine law which is the law of grace does not do away with human law which is based on the law of natural reason'.[133] For Grotius, this implies that the obligations and rights that belong to primary and secondary natural law apply irrespective of religious differences. In other words: under natural law, the believers can have rights and obligations even towards those with 'false' religious beliefs, such as non-Christians and heretics.

While in the first premise, Grotius emphasizes natural law's independence of religion (so that natural rights and obligations apply irrespective of religious 'error'), his second premise seems to point into the opposite direction: the believers must 'carefully guard against all things that appear to go against divine glory and the true religion'.[134] It is unclear whether Grotius's second premise was also inspired by Aquinas, who had emphasized the duty of the believers to avoid any relations with non-Christians that could provoke a scandal and endanger the faith. Aquinas had specifically warned against the risk of apostasy, i.e., the risk of Christians 'falling away' from the true religion—a risk that existed especially in *unequal* relations, if Christians became the servants or subjects of non-Christian masters or rulers.[135] In his second premise, Grotius does not mention Aquinas, but instead refers to the Gospel itself: 'first of all, seek the kingdom of heaven'.[136] Although the believers can have natu-

---

and the law of nations: Haggenmacher, *Grotius et la doctrine de la guerre juste*, pp. 329–399; Randall Lesaffer, 'Grotius on Reprisal', *Grotiana*, 41 (2020), 330–348 (p. 345).

131 *IPC*, ed. Hamaker, p. 12, ed. Van Ittersum, p. 25; Lesaffer, 'Grotius on Reprisal', p. 345.

132 Grotius, *De societate*, fol. 314^r, prem. 1.

133 *S. Th.* 2a 2ae, q. 10, a. 10, resp.: 'Ius autem divinum, quod est ex gratia, non tollit ius humanum, quod est ex naturali ratione'. Aquinas had developed this argument in response to the question whether non-believers (*infideles*) could exercise dominion or authority over the believers. In Aquinas's opinion, non-believers were not allowed to establish dominion or authority over the believers, as it could lead to apostasy: the believers could thus be forced or induced to adopt their masters' non-Christian faith. However, if the authority or dominion of the non-believers over the faithful had *already* been established, it had to be respected, since divine law did not do away with the human laws of ownership and authority which originated from natural reason.

134 Grotius, *De societate*, fol. 314^r, prem. 2.

135 *S. Th.* 2a 2ae, q. 10, a. 10, resp.

136 Math. 6.33; Grotius, *De societate*, fol. 314^r, prem. 2.

ral rights and obligations towards non-believers, they have an overriding duty to protect the Christian faith.[137] The same verse from Matthew is later quoted and explained in *De iure belli ac pacis*: 'No right whatsoever is sufficient to warrant committing what will probably be harmful to religion, indirectly, if not directly. For as a matter of first importance the kingdom of heaven is to be sought, that is, the spread of the Gospel'.[138] Hence, no man-made or natural law may be invoked against the true religion, and the believers, instead, have a duty to contribute to the propagation of the Gospel. According to Grotius, alliances with non-Christians should thus be avoided if 'the power of the heathen' is thereby 'greatly increased'.[139] The reason is that if non-Christian rulers become too powerful, it may hinder the spread of the Gospel.

The combination of Grotius's first and second premises implies that public and private partnerships between Christians and non-Christians are *in general* permissible under natural and divine law, *unless* they entail the risk of undermining the authority of God and the Christian religion. For Grotius, the defense of the true religion and the spread of the Gospel prevail over profane interests. However, this does not mean that Grotius reduces 'the possibility of making alliances with the infidels to a mere theoretical possibility', as one legal historian recently argued.[140] Instead, in Grotius's view, whether or not alliances with non-Christians are permissible depends on the nature of these alliances: if they greatly increase the power of non-Christian nations, then they may hinder the spread of the Gospel and must be avoided. By contrast, if alliances with nonbelievers increase the power of Christian nations, then they can effectively support the spread of the Gospel and contribute to the conversion of the 'infidels' to the Christian faith. More particularly, while alliances with non-Christians can deepen the internal divisions of Christianity in the European context,[141] Grotius believes they can strengthen the position of Christian nations in the non-European context. As he concludes in *De iure praedae*, by entering into alliances with East-Indian rulers and by protecting the 'infidels' from harm, the

137 Cf. Condorelli, 'Grotius's Doctrine of Alliances with Infidels', p. 29.

138 *IBP*, II.15.11 (trans. Kelsey, p. 403).

139 *IBP*, II.15.11.2.

140 Condorelli, 'Grotius's Doctrine of Alliances with Infidels', p. 29.

141 For instance, the sixteenth-century alliances between France and the Ottoman Empire had deepened divisions between France and the Habsburg empire, as well as between the Valois kings and their Huguenot subjects (who were strongly opposed to the alliance with the Ottomans). See Édith Garnier, *L'alliance impie: François 1er et Soliman le Magnifique contre Charles V* (Paris: Éditions du Félin, 2008) and Tuck, 'Alliances with Infidels', pp. 66–67 and 71. On Grotius's perception of the threat of the Ottoman Empire, see Condorelli, 'Grotius's Doctrine of Alliances with Infidels', pp. 31–32.

Dutch had effectively contributed to the spread of the Gospel: 'there is nothing that serves the cause of the true religion better than such acts of kindness ... Let them [the Indians, MdW] marvel at the faith which forbids that even unbelievers should be neglected. In achieving these ends, we shall be preparing men for God'.[142]

According to Grotius, it is thus generally permitted for Christians to enter into alliances with non-Christians, provided that these alliances do not undermine the Christian faith or hinder the spread of the Gospel. However, as Grotius emphasizes in the third premise of *De societate*, even if something is generally permitted, it is still necessary to distinguish what is decent from what is offending: in other words, even if a particular course of action is *legally* permissible, it is not always *morally* justified.[143] Whether or not a particular course of action is justified depends on the circumstances of the case. According to Grotius's fourth premise, in cases of 'extreme necessity' (*extrema necessitas*) many things become lawful which are otherwise unlawful.[144] For instance, although Christians are generally prohibited from submitting themselves to the authority of a non-Christian ruler (because they can then be forced or induced to apostasy), this may become permissible in cases of necessity, if it is the only way to preserve one's life.[145] Moreover, according to Grotius's fifth premise, what is normally just can cease to be just, and vice versa, due to a 'special vocation' (i.e., a divine calling).[146] Grotius refers to the biblical example of Esther who—in violation of the general prohibition on mixed marriages between the faithful and non-believers—was 'perhaps' called to marry an infidel husband, because it allowed her to reveal the plot against her people.[147] Finally, according to Grotius's sixth premise, many actions that are just in themselves can become

142 *IPC*, ed. Hamaker, p. 299, ed. Van Ittersum, p. 435.

143 Grotius, *De societate*, fol. 314r, prem. 3.

144 Ibid., fol. 314r, prem. 4.

145 Ibid., fol. 317v, prop. 9. Legal exceptions that are justified by 'extreme necessity' play an important role in *De iure belli ac pacis*, for instance, in the second chapter of book 2 dealing with the right to use someone else's possessions in cases of necessity: thus, if a man under the stress of necessity takes from another what is necessary to preserve his own life, he does not commit theft, because 'in times of necessity, all things become common [*in tempore necessitatis omnia sunt communia*]'. Grotius formulates several conditions for accepting necessity as a justification for behavior that is otherwise unlawful: the necessity should be evident, urgent, unavoidable, and property should be restored to the original owner after the necessity has passed. See *IBP*, II.2.6–10.

146 Grotius, *De societate*, fol. 314r, prem. 5. On exceptions *ex vocatione speciale* see also Grotius, *Commentarius in Theses XI*, ed. Borschberg, pp. 208–209 and note 745.

147 Cf. Esth. 2.16–17. Grotius, *De societate*, fol. 315v, prop. 5, lim.

unjust if they are done with the wrong intent.[148] In *De societate*, Grotius does not give any specific examples, but one may think of the case in which the believers enter into an alliance with non-Christians merely as a pretext to wage an unjustified war against another Christian nation.[149]

In his seventh premise, Grotius distinguishes between two categories of 'non-believers:' those who belong to the church and those who do not.[150] Elsewhere in *De societate*, he explains this distinction: 'It should be noted here that there are two kinds of non-believers or *ἑτεροδόξοι*; those who never belonged to the Church; and those who departed from it, or are expelled by an ecclesiastical judgement'.[151] As we have seen, the first category includes Jews, Muslims and 'pagans'. The second relates to heretics and apostates. To justify these distinctions Grotius refers to a verse from Paul's first letter to the Corinthians: 'For what have I to do to judge them also that are without? Do not ye judge them that are within'.[152] This verse from Paul had played an important role in sixteenth-century debates about whether the pope could exercise jurisdiction over non-Christian populations.[153] For instance, in his lecture on the American 'Indians', the Spanish jurist-theologian Francisco de Vitoria had referred to 1 Cor. 5.12 to argue that the pope had no spiritual power over the 'infidel' nations of the Americas and that, consequently, he did not have any temporal power over them either.[154] It was thus unjustified to wage war against the American 'Indians' merely because they refused to accept papal authority or the Christian

148 Ibid., fol. 314r, prem. 6.

149 This is not an arbitrary example: the requirement of righteous intention played an important role in medieval and early-modern discourses about the laws of war. Aquinas had identified 'righteous intention [*recta intentio*]' as one of the three main conditions for a war to be just, along with 'sovereignty [*auctoritas principis*]' and 'just cause [*causa iusta*]'. In *De iure belli ac pacis*, Grotius emphasized that a war could only be lawfully undertaken with a righteous intention, that is, with an earnest intention to restore peace. On the criterion of righteous intention in Aquinas and Grotius, see, e.g., Haggenmacher, *Grotius et la doctrine de la guerre juste*, pp. 166 and 400 ff. and Randall Lesaffer, 'The Laws of War- and Peace-Making', in *The Cambridge Companion to Hugo Grotius*, pp. 433–456 (pp. 435 and 441).

150 Grotius, *De societate*, fol. 314r, prem 7.

151 Ibid., fol. 315v, in p[ropositione]m.

152 1 Cor. 5.12. Cf. ibid., fol. 315v.

153 See, inter alia, David M. Lantigua, *Infidels and Empires in a New World Order: Early Modern Spanish Contributions to International Legal Thought* (Cambridge: Cambridge University Press, 2020), p. 126.

154 Francisco de Vitoria, *De Indis insulanis relectio prior*, in Vitoria, *Relectiones theologicae XII* (Lugduni: Apud Iacobum Boyerium, 1557), q. 2, a. 2, § 30. Translated as Vitoria, 'On the American Indians', in *Political Writings*, ed. and trans. by Anthony Pagden and Jeremy Lawrance (Cambridge: Cambridge University Press, 2010), pp. 231–292 (pp. 262–263).

faith.[155] Only if the Indians had converted to Christianity and become members of the ecclesiastical community did they fall under the pope's jurisdiction.[156] In *De iure praedae*, Grotius applied Vitoria's arguments to the East-Indian context, arguing that the princes and nations of the East Indies could not be deprived of their lands on the mere ground that the pope as 'lord of the East Indies' had donated their lands to the Spaniards and Portuguese. As Grotius concluded, it was clear that 'even the Saracens were never despoiled on such grounds'.[157]

In his eighth premise, Grotius distinguishes between the different types of 'societies' that can exist between the believers and non-believers: they can either be public or private, equal or unequal, superior or inferior.[158] 'Public societies' are entered into by, or on behalf of, states or public authorities (e.g., treaties or alliances between states). By contrast, 'private societies' refer to contracts or agreements between private parties (e.g., commercial contracts or business associations). As we have seen, in practice, the distinction between public and private societies was not always clear: for instance, in its founding charter, the VOC had been authorized to enter into alliances with foreign rulers on behalf of the Dutch Estates General—these alliances were considered *public* alliances, even though they had been initiated by a *private* trading company.[159] Moreover, Grotius explains that alliances between the believers and non-believers can either be equal or unequal, in the sense that they confer equal or unequal rights on the parties involved. In his *Theses XI*, Grotius had given the example of an 'unequal alliance' that granted the superior party the right to impose taxes upon its subject-ally, while allowing its ally self-government in other respects.[160] Grotius would further develop his theory about 'unequal alliances' in *De iure belli ac pacis*.[161] Here he explained that unequal alliances imposed 'temporary or permanent burdens' on the weaker party in exchange for protection by the superior party.[162] As Grotius empha-

155 Vitoria, *De Indis*, q. 2, a. 4, § 39.

156 Ibid., q. 3, a. 3, § 13.

157 *IPC*, ed. Hamaker, p. 211, ed. Van Ittersum, p. 311.

158 Grotius, *De societate*, fol. 314^r, prem. 8.

159 Charter of the VOC. In *Groot Placaet-Boeck vervattende de placaten, ordonnantien en edicten van de doorluchtige, Hoogh Moghende Heeren Staten-Generael der Vereenighde Nederlanden*, ed. Cornelis Cau (The Hague: Van Wouw, 1658), p. 536.

160 As Grotius explained, the subject-ally maintained the right to make its own laws and control its own courts, even if it had lost the right of taxation. Grotius, *Theses XI*, ed. Borschberg, p. 233, sub 29.

161 *IBP*, II.15.7. Grotius presents his theory about unequal treaties in a section preceding the one on alliances with non-Christians.

162 *IBP*, II.15.7.3.

sized, the weaker party did not thereby necessarily lose its sovereignty. However, if unequal alliances became perpetual and if they granted the superior party the right to place garrisons on the lands of the inferior party, they could eventually lead to a transfer of sovereignty.[163] This happened in the East Indies, where the VOC's alliances with East-Indian rulers often forced the latter to vow 'perpetual' allegiance to the Dutch, while allowing them to build fortresses on native soil.[164]

According to Grotius's ninth premise, an 'alliance for purposes of war' (*societas bellica*) can be justified as well.[165] Both in the main text and in the reading notes of *De societate*, Grotius refers to the distinction made by Thucydides between two kinds of military alliances: *συμμαχία* and *ἐπιμαχία*.[166] While the first relates to alliances established with a view to any cause of war whatsoever, the second pertains only to defensive alliances. Grotius had made the same distinction in *De iure praedae*, where he had connected the right to enter into defensive alliances (*ἐπιμαχία*) to the first law of nature: the right to defend one's life and to shun what threatened to prove injurious.[167] Grotius would further elaborate on Thucydides's distinction in *De iure belli ac pacis*, where he explained that the term *συμμαχία* referred to general alliances by which parties agreed to have the 'same enemies and friends', while the term *ἐπιμαχία* stood for alliances aimed at protecting the parties' boundaries only.[168] In both the reading notes of *De societate* and *De iure belli ac pacis*, Grotius refers to alliances (*foedera*) between the Romans and their *socii* mentioned by Livy as examples of *συμμαχία*.[169] However, as Grotius warns in his tenth premise, not every alliance between the believers and the non-believers can be just: what is permissible in general is not always just. As Grotius formulates it, 'universal [alliance] should not be just without exception'.[170] Whether or not an alliance

163 *IBP*, I.3.21.10.

164 An example is the VOC's treaty with the rulers of the Banda islands of 10 August 1609, which forced the latter to recognize the VOC's right to build a fortress on the island of Banda Neira and to hold it 'in perpetuity' (*eeuwelijck ende erffelijck*). The treaty can be found in F.W. Stapel, 'Corpus diplomaticum Neerlando-Indicum', pp. 66–69 (p. 68) (XXX). On Grotius's theory of unequal alliances and the role it played in justifying Dutch expansion in the East Indies, see Inge van Hulle, 'Grotius, Informal Empire and the Conclusion of Unequal Treaties', *Grotiana*, 37 (2016), pp. 43–60.

165 Grotius, *De societate*, fol. 314^{r}, prem. 9.

166 The reference is to Thuc. 1.41.149. In Grotius, *De societate*, fol. 314^{r} (main text), 316 (2)^{v} (reading notes) and 317^{r} (main text).

167 *IPC*, ed. Hamaker, p. 65, ed. Van Ittersum, p. 100. Cf. *IBP*, II.15.6.3.

168 *IBP*, II.15.6.3.

169 *IBP*, II.15.6.3 and Grotius, *De societate*, fol. 316 (2)^{v}. The reference is to Liv. 23.35.3.

170 Grotius, *De societate*, fol. 314^{r}, prem. 10.

with non-Christians is just depends on the circumstances. For instance, military alliances with non-Christians can only be just if either the believers or the non-believers have a just cause for war (e.g., if they have been unjustly attacked by others). Most importantly, as we have seen, alliances with non-Christians cannot be just if they risk undermining the authority of God or the Christian faith. Instead, for Grotius, the legitimacy of alliances with non-believers ultimately depends on whether they contribute to, or hinder, the spread of the Gospel.

7.2 *Propositions and Conclusions*

7.2.1 General Principles: Preventing Harm and Cultivating Friendship

After presenting his ten premises, Grotius continues by formulating a set of general propositions relating to the various kinds of partnerships between Christians and non-Christians (e.g., private and public, equal and unequal, etc.). His first proposition is that '[t]o refrain from harming non-believers and heretics in general is not only permissible for Christians, but also necessary'.[171] As Grotius indicates, this proposition follows from the first premise, according to which an 'error of faith' does not diminish the obligations that originate from the law of nature. The law to which Grotius refers in his first proposition is the natural law of non-offensiveness, which prescribes that one should refrain from harming others without cause. In *De iure praedae*, Grotius had identified several sources of this law, including Justinian's *Institutes* and Cicero's *De officiis*, which described the obligation to refrain from harming others, unless provoked by wrong, as a fundamental duty of justice.[172] In both *De iure praedae* and *De societate*, Grotius suggests that the duty to refrain from harming others without cause is a fundamental duty under natural law, which applies independently of religion: hence, in general, Christians should refrain from harming others, including non-believers and heretics. As Grotius explains in *De societate*, the natural law of non-offensiveness does not conflict with Christian law, but is instead confirmed by it: 'the law of nature prescribes that evil should be inflicted on no one, and Christ emphasizes this a thousand times'.[173] In Grotius's opinion, Christians therefore have a duty under natural *and* Christian law to refrain from harming others, including non-Christians and heretics.

From this first proposition, Grotius derives his first conclusion: 'It is permissible for both private and public persons to enter into a pact with non-believers

171 Ibid., fol. 314^{v}, prop. 1.

172 Cic. *off.* 1.7.20 and *Inst.* 1.1.3. The same law can be found in the *Dig.* 1.1.10.1. *IPC*, ed. Hamaker, pp. 13–14, ed. Van Ittersum, p. 27 (third law).

173 Grotius, *De societate*, fol. 314^{v}, prop. 1.

or heretics not to harm one another'.[174] To justify his conclusion, Grotius refers to the examples of the alliances of Abraham and Isaac with the 'heathen King' Abimelech, the alliance of Jacob with his father-in-law Laban, and of David and Solomon with Hiram, the king of Tyre.[175] These same examples are also mentioned in the reading notes, where they are briefly explained.[176] For instance, the alliance between the 'pious man' Abraham and the 'heathen king' Abimelech is characterized by Grotius as an alliance 'of non-offensiveness and of cultivating friendship'.[177] However, alliances to prevent harm are not always permissible. Grotius makes an exception for those cases in which the believers have been expressly forbidden by God to enter into pacts or alliances with particular infidel peoples. He gives the examples of the Amalekites and the 'six cursed peoples', who were condemned by a divine sentence:[178] the believers were thus required by a divine decree to punish these 'infidel' peoples and strictly prohibited from entering into an alliance with them.[179] Even so, Grotius warns his readers not to confuse the exception with the rule: the believers are not allowed to enter into alliances with the Amalekites and the 'six cursed peoples' due to a 'special reason', but in general, it is permissible for the believers to enter into alliances with non-believers to protect each other from harm. In *De iure belli ac pacis*, Grotius refers to the same biblical examples to conclude that, generally speaking, alliances 'with those who are strangers to the true religion [*cum his qui a vera religione alieni sunt*]' are permissible under Hebraic law.[180]

While Grotius's first proposition relates to alliances to prevent harm, his second pertains to treaties of friendship and commercial partnerships: 'Good deeds, duties, trades, for the sake of charity, civility, and utility, can be rightly cultivated reciprocally between the faithful and the non-believers or heretics'.[181] The right to cultivate friendship with non-believers follows from Grotius's first premise, according to which 'errors of faith' do not change the law

174 Ibid., fol. 314ᵛ, concl. 1.

175 Gen. 21.27, 26.29, and 31.49; 2 Sam. 5.11, 5.12, and 1 Reg. 9.11–12. These examples are mentioned in Grotius, *De societate*, fol. 314ᵛ, sub concl. 1.

176 Grotius, *De societate*, fol. 316 (1)ʳ.

177 Ibid., fol. 316 (1)ʳ.

178 Ex. 17.16 and Deut. 25.17 (reference to the Amalekites) and Deut. 7.1 (reference to seven peoples that are condemned) or Ex. 34.11 (reference to six peoples that are condemned).

179 Grotius, *De societate*, fol. 314ᵛ, exception to concl. 1. The same examples are mentioned in the reading notes: fol. 316 (1)ʳ.

180 *IBP*, II.15.9.1 (the treaties between Jacob and Laban, and between Abraham and Isaac and Abimelech, and the divine decree relating to the Amelekites and six (or seven) cursed peoples) and II.15.9.2 (the treaties of David and Solomon with Hiram).

181 Grotius, *De societate*, fol. 314ᵛ, prop. 2.

of nature. Once again, natural law is confirmed by divine law: the reading notes refer to several examples of kings of Israel who had concluded treaties of friendship or trade with non-believers: for instance, the alliance between Abraham and Abimelech is characterized by Grotius as an alliance for 'cultivating friendship [*societas de colenda amicitia*]' and the alliance between Solomon and Hiram as a 'partnership for trade [*societas mercatoria*]'.[182] Grotius's proposition is, moreover, followed by an important amplification: 'it is not only allowed to do good to non-believers or heretics, but according to the circumstances ... even necessary, when we can help them without great disadvantage to ourselves, especially when they ask our help themselves'.[183] In other words: the faithful not only have a *right*, but, depending on the circumstances, also a *duty* to do good to non-believers. Grotius gives the example of showing a stranger the way to a well, which should be regarded as a 'duty of civility' (*officium civilitatis*), but which may turn into a legal obligation in case of 'extreme necessity' (e.g., if the stranger would otherwise die from thirst).[184]

To prove his second proposition that the believers should do good to non-believers and heretics, Grotius refers to classical and biblical sources. He mentions Cicero's discussion of Ennius, who had given the example of showing a stranger the way and allowing him to lit his lamp with one's own.[185] Cicero had related the duty 'to bestow even upon a stranger what it costs us nothing to give' to natural law, arguing that 'the common right to all things nature has produced for the common use of man is to be maintained'.[186] In *De iure praedae*, Grotius had referred to the same passage in Cicero, explaining that 'everything capable of serving the convenience of a given person without detriment of the interests of any other person' had remained the 'common possession of all'.[187] Grotius had given the examples of the sea and running water: even when used by a specific individual or nation, they nevertheless sufficed for general use by others: hence, under the law of nature, a right of use existed to whatever was suitable to being used by all, and, since it originated from nature itself, it applied independently of religion. In *De societate*, Grotius refers not only to Cicero, but also to Seneca's opinion that good should be done even to the wicked and the ungrateful.[188] In *De beneficiis* (4.28), Seneca had observed that God 'has given

182 Ibid., fol. 316 (1)^r^.
183 Ibid., fol. 314^v^.
184 Ibid., fol. 315^r^.
185 Cic. *off.* 1.16.51.
186 Cic. *off.* 1.16.51.
187 IPC, ed. Hamaker, p. 218, ed. Van Ittersum, p. 321 (with a reference to Cic. *off.* 1.16.51).
188 Grotius, *De societate*, fol. 315^r^.

certain gifts to the whole human race, and from these no man is shut out'.[189] He had mentioned the sea as an example: it was 'to the common good that traffic on the sea should be open to all'.[190] As Grotius suggests in *De societate*, the principles formulated by Cicero and Seneca apply to all 'benefits': hence, under natural law, 'gifts, services, favours' should be bestowed on the believers as well as on non-believers and heretics.[191]

According to Grotius, the duty to do good to non-believers and heretics does not only follow from natural law, but also from Christian law. He evokes the parable of the Samaritan, explaining that Christ thereby instructed the Jews to treat others as their neighbours.[192] He also quotes a verse from Juvenal's *Satires* to criticize the 'errors of the Jews', which allegedly consisted of their refusal to provide assistance to non-believers.[193] The same combination of sources reappears in the introduction of Grotius's *Remonstrantie*, where he explains that 'the Jews have held the malicious view that they do not owe people of other religions even the smallest acts of kindness, to which our Lord bears witness in the parable of the Samaritan, which taught, contrary to Jewish opinion, that the expression "our neighbours" must not be restricted to members of the same religion. A Roman poet who described the Jewish customs said they would not want to show the way nor a well to an uncircumcised man'.[194] Refuting this 'malicious view' of the Jews, Grotius explains that the parable of the Samaritan teaches the believers to treat all people as their neighbours, including those of other creeds.[195] The implication is that 'non-believers' (including the Jews themselves) should be treated well, despite their 'errors'. To support his conclusion Grotius quotes the Sermon on the Mount: 'Do like your Father, who causes his sun to rise and sends his rain on the good and the evil'.[196] The same quotation can be found in *De societate*, where Grotius explains that the sun and the rain stand for 'all the good things of Nature'.[197] In *De societate* and the *Remonstrantie*, the same sources (e.g., the verses from Juvenal's *Satires*, the parable of the Samaritan, and the Sermon on the Mount) are invoked to

189 Sen. *ben.* 4.28.
190 Sen. *ben.* 4.28.
191 Grotius, *De societate*, fol. 315r, with reference to Sen. *ben.* 4.29.
192 Grotius refers to Ioh. 4.9, Luc. 10.36 and Act. 10.28; Grotius, *De societate*, fol. 314v.
193 Juv. *Sat.* 14.103–104; Grotius, *De societate*, fol. 314v.
194 Grotius, *Remonstrantie*, fol. 2r–2v, pp. 63–65, trans., p. 199, with reference to Juv. *Sat.* on fol. 2v.
195 Ibid., fol. 6v, p. 80–81, trans., p. 202.
196 Math. 5.45, quoted in ibid., fol. 6v, pp. 80–81, trans., p. 202.
197 Grotius, *De societate*, fol. 315r.

demonstrate that the believers should treat non-Christians (e.g., Jews) well.[198] As Grotius suggests, this is not merely a right, but a legal and religious obligation.[199]

However, according to Grotius, the duty to do good to non-believers is subject to three conditions (or 'limitations'), which follow from his second premise. The first is that '[g]reater charity must be shown towards the faithful than towards the unfaithful'.[200] As evidence for his claim Grotius refers to Paul's Letter to the Galatians: 'Let us do good unto all men, especially unto them who are of the [same] household of faith'.[201] The question whether in doing good to others the believers should be preferred over non-believers had been the topic of an age-old theological debate, which had focused on the issue of alms-giving. In his reading notes, Grotius refers to Aquinas's discussion of whether the believers should give preference to their fellow-believers in alms-giving.[202] Aquinas had concluded that, as a general rule, Christians should in preference help their fellow-believers. However, they had discretion in determining whom to give alms to, according to the various degrees of connection, holiness and utility.[203] This implied that they could decide to prioritize, for instance, those in greater want over those more closely connected to them. Moreover, later scholastics argued that in cases of necessity, when receiving alms was necessary to preserve one's life, no distinction could be made between the believers and non-believers.[204] For instance, in his *Deliberatio in causa pauperum* (1545), the Dominican theologian Domingo de Soto concluded that 'if the matter is referred higher, to natural law, the human race is united by the closest bond

---

198 The same references (including Juvenal, the parable of the Samaritan, the Sermon on the Mount), although not in the same order, can be found in *IBP*, II.15.9 and 10.

199 Conversely, Grotius argues that Christians should accept the good deeds of non-believers. He refers to Christ himself, who accepted a drink of water from a Samaritan woman, and to the Apostle Paul, who was protected by the Romans. Citing 1 Cor. 10.27, he adds that if Christians are invited by 'infidels' for dinner, they should go and eat whatever is offered to them. He explains that this, too, was against Jewish institutions, since the Jews blamed Christ for attending banquets with non-believers. Unlike the Jews, the believers should accept benefits from the non-believers, and they are allowed to trade with them. Grotius, *De societate*, fol. 315^r.

200 Grotius, *De societate*, 315^r, lim. 1.

201 Gal. 6.10.

202 *S. Th.* 2 2ae, q. 32, a. 9. The reference can be found in Grotius, *De societate*, fol. 316 (2)^r: 'Eleemosyna an propinquioribus facienda an peccatori[bus]' ('Whether alms should be given to those to whom we are more closely related or to sinners').

203 *S. Th.* 2 2ae, q. 32, a. 9 resp.

204 Annabel Brett, *Changes of State: Nature and the Limits of the City in Early Modern Natural Law* (Cambridge: Cambridge University Press, 2011), pp. 11–36 (pp. 29–30).

in its very nature, so that, unless they were our enemies, or we feared some detriment to the faith from them, it would not be rightful to reject even infidel beggars from our commonwealth'.[205]

One of the conditions for alms-giving to 'infidel beggars' mentioned by Soto—that no alms may be given to 'infidel beggars' if it causes some detriment to the faith—reappears in Grotius's second limitation: it is not allowed to bestow charity on non-believers if it entails the risk of causing a loss of faith.[206] As Grotius indicates, this limitation follows from the second premise that the believers should avoid anything that may diminish the glory of God and the true religion.[207] Grotius illustrates the limitation with the example of usury. Under the laws of the church, the believers were strictly forbidden from practicing usury, that is, from lending money on interest.[208] However, the prohibition did not apply to strangers: it was thus permissible to take usury from strangers.[209] As Aquinas explained, taking usury from strangers was not in general lawful, but it was permissible to avoid a greater evil, namely that avarice might lead the believers to take usury from their fellow-believers.[210] From a Christian perspective, usury and infidelity were closely related: usury was regarded as the economic manifestation of various forms of infidelity, and as the consequence of the incapacity of non-believers (e.g., Jews) to recognize the spiritual value of Scripture.[211] Grotius does not mention Aquinas in this context, but he quotes directly from the Bible: 'You shall lend to a stranger at usury; but not to your brother. You shall demand [usury] from a foreigner'.[212] Explaining these verses, Grotius notes that the community that exists between men by nature (*societas naturae*) is limited by the community between the faithful that exists by divine grace (*societas gratiae*).[213] Therefore, Grotius believes it is reasonable to give preference to the faithful over non-believers, and to accept usury from strangers, but not from brothers.

---

205 Domingo de Soto, *Deliberatio in causa pauperum* (Salmantiae: Ioannes Maria a Terranova, 1566), cap. 4, fol. 103 (trans. in Brett, *Changes of State*, pp. 29–30).

206 Grotius, *De societate*, fol. 315^r, lim. 2.

207 Ibid., fol. 314^r, prem. 2.

208 See, e.g., Grat. *Decr.* C. 14, q. 3 and 4.

209 Deut. 23.19.

210 *S. Th.* 2 2ae, q. 78, a. 1, resp. ad 2.

211 On the connection between usury and infidelity: Giacomo Todeschini, 'The Incivility of Judas: "Manifest" Usury as a Metaphor for the "Infamy of Fact" (*infamia facti*)', in *Money, Morality, and Culture in Late Medieval and Early Modern Europe*, ed. by Juliann Vitullo and Diana Wolfthal (London: Routledge, 2010), pp. 33–52.

212 Deut. 15.3; Grotius, *De societate*, fol. 315^r, prop. 2, lim. 2.

213 Ibid., fol. 315^r, prop. 2, lim. 2.

Having discussed the duty to do good (e.g., to give alms) to non-believers, Grotius examines the various types of private and public 'societies' that may exist between the believers and non-believers. He begins by presenting his views on 'equal societies', which may testify to 'different degrees' of friendship and familiarity.[214] Changing the order of presentation, he starts by outlining the limitations to his third proposition before formulating the proposition itself. The first limitation is that stronger bonds of friendship and familiarity should be cultivated with the faithful than with non-believers. Grotius explains that the 'greatest bond of friendship [*maximum amicitiae vinculum*]' is the 'harmony of strivings [*studiorum consensio*], especially concerning the greatest matters [*res maximas*]'.[215] Grotius seems to refer to Cicero's speech on behalf of Gnaeus Plancius, where the Roman philosopher identifies the 'complete unity of aim' as the 'traditional condition of genuine and sincere friendship'. As Cicero specifies, 'there is no surer bond of friendship [*amicitiae vinculum*] than the sympathetic union of thought and inclination [*consensus et societas consiliorum et voluntatum*]'.[216] By relating Cicero's concept of friendship to the 'greatest matters', Grotius reinterprets it in religious terms, as the bond that exists between the believers. With a reference to Aristotle and the Gospel, he suggests that the 'harmony of strivings' is based on brotherly love (*φιλαδελφία*) and aimed towards divine truth.[217] The implication is that stronger bonds of friendship and familiarity should exist between the believers than between the believers and non-believers.[218]

Recalling the distinction from his seventh premise, Grotius points out that there are two kinds of non-believers: those who never belonged to the Church (i.e., non-Christians), and those who departed from it or were expelled from it by an ecclesiastical judgement (i.e., apostates and heretics).[219] From this premise follows a second limitation: the believers should in general abstain

214 Ibid., fol. 315ᵛ, after the third limitation: 'III. Lim[itatio] ex III p[rae]m[isso/issione]'.

215 Ibid., fol. 315ʳ, prop. 3, lim. 1.

216 Cic. *Planc.* 2.5: 'and indeed there is no surer bond of friendship than the sympathetic union of thought and inclination [*consensus et societas consiliorum et voluntatum*]' (trans. Neville Hunter Watts). See also Cic. *amic.* 4.15, where he defines friendship as 'the most complete agreement in policy, in pursuits, and in opinions [*voluntatum studiorum sententiarum summa consensio*]' (trans. William Armistead Falconer).

217 Aristot. *eth. Nic.* 1156b, 1157a, and 1158ab.

218 A similar argument can be found in Grotius's *Remonstrantie*: '[w]hen the apostle Paul enjoins us to be good to all people, in particular our fellow believers, he does presume a closer bond between the believers, but does not exclude the unbelievers from the bond of love'. Grotius, *Remonstrantie*, fol. 6ᵛ, pp. 80–81, trans., p. 202.

219 Grotius, *De societate*, fol. 315ᵛ.

from intimate relations and social intercourse with those who have left the church or who have been condemned by its judgement.[220] According to Grotius, there is a 'special reason' for not associating with heretics and apostates: they should 'return to shame and repentance'.[221] However, the duty to abstain from associating with apostates and heretics does not apply without exceptions: in cases of necessity, it is allowed to associate with them.[222] According to Grotius, this is also permissible in cases of utility if the believers associate with the non-believers in the hope of converting them to the true faith. However, in a deleted sentence, Grotius suggests that the exception does not apply to those believers who are of weak conviction: they should abstain from intimate relations with 'other non-believers', because they thereby risk falling away from the faith themselves.[223] In *De iure belli ac pacis*, Grotius makes a similar observation with regard to 'strangers to the true religion:' he argues that 'too great intimacy' with the latter should be avoided, because it may contribute to a 'contamination of the weak'.[224] For this reason, the believers should live apart from non-believers, just as the Israelites lived apart from the Egyptians during their exile.[225] Likewise, in his *Remonstrantie*, Grotius observes that the mere sight of the Jews may 'instill doubts in the weak-minded regarding the principal points of salvation'.[226] However, he also suggests that this can be prevented by good legislation and the efforts of the clergy.[227]

220 Ibid., fol. 315^{v}, prop. 3, lim. 2.

221 Grotius refers to a verse in Titus, which requires the believers to reject heretics and apostates after they have been admonished for the second time. Tit. 3.10, in ibid. 315^{v}.

222 Grotius, *De societate*, fol. 315^{v}, prop. 3, lim. 2. See also the reading notes on fol. 316 (1)^{r}, right column: 'Quatenus media alias non licita ex necessitate fiunt licita'.

223 Grotius, *De societate*, fol. 315^{v}, prop. 3, lim. 2. The sentence has been crossed out with two diagonal lines. The words are still clearly visible. It is unclear why Grotius decided to delete this particular sentence. Perhaps, he decided to remove the sentence for political reasons. There are other examples of sentences that Grotius later removed from his manuscripts because of political sensitivities. For instance, Martine van Ittersum has showed that, in the Winter of 1608, Grotius erased all references to Spanish claims in the Americas from the manuscript of *Mare liberum* (chapter 12 of *De iure praedae*). This was deemed necessary in view of the ongoing negotiations about a truce agreement between the Dutch Republic and Spain. As a protégé of Johan van Oldenbarnevelt, Grotius wanted to prevent his treatise from unnecessarily offending the Spanish negotiators. Martine van Ittersum, 'Preparing *Mare liberum* for the Press: Hugo Grotius' Rewriting of Chapter 12 of *De iure praedae* in November–December 1608', *Grotiana*, 26–28 (2005–2007), 246–280 (at p. 259–261 and 273).

224 *IBP*, II.15.9.1.

225 *IBP*, II.15.9.1.

226 Grotius, *Remonstrantie*, fol. 2^{r}, pp. 62–63, trans., p. 199.

227 Ibid., fol. 8^{v}, pp. 88–89, trans., p. 203.

The source of Grotius's second limitation appears to be Aquinas's discussion of whether the believers are allowed to 'communicate' with non-believers.[228] As Aquinas explains, there are two reasons why it may be forbidden for the believers to communicate with non-believers. The first is to punish non-believers for their unbelief. The second is to protect the believers from the risk that they may be led away from the faith. Crucially, the first reason (punishment) applies only to non-believers who have forsaken the faith they once received, either by corrupting it, as heretics, or by renouncing it, as apostates: the believers are thus forbidden from communicating with heretics and apostates so that they are punished for corrupting or renouncing the Christian faith.[229] By contrast, it is not forbidden for the believers to communicate with non-believers who have never received or accepted the Christian faith, such as Jews and pagans. The latter may not be punished for their lack of faith, because the church does not exercise any spiritual judgement over them (as they do not belong to the Christian community). However, as Aquinas explains, the believers may not communicate with Jews or pagans if they thereby risk falling away from the faith themselves. Hence, those believers who are 'firm in their faith' may communicate with Jews and pagans in the hope of converting them to Christianity. However, 'simple people, who are weak in their faith, and whose perversion is to be feared as a probable result, should be forbidden from communicating with non-believers, and especially from being on very familiar terms with them, or from communicating with them without necessity'.[230]

Grotius's second limitation builds on these distinctions: it applies specifically to heretics and apostates, but not to Jews and pagans. The believers should thus refrain from living together or associating with apostates and heretics for a 'special reason', namely 'that they should return to shame and repentance'.[231] By contrast, Grotius's third limitation applies to both heretics and apostates, and non-Christians, such as pagans and Jews. The believers are thus warned 'not to enter into a very close familiarity with non-believers and heretics without reason, but those who converse with non-believers of another kind should take care on all occasions, so that they try to bring them to good sense both by doctrine and example'.[232] The final part of the sentence is essential: it implies that no force may be used to convert non-believers to Christianity. Instead, the

228 *S. Th.* 2 2ae, q. 10, a. 9: 'utrum cum infidelibus possit communicari'.
229 *S. Th.* 2 2ae, q. 10, a. 9, resp.
230 *S. Th.* 2 2ae, q. 10, a. 9, resp.
231 Grotius, *De societate*, fol. 315^v, prop. 3, lim 2.
232 Ibid., fol. 315^v, lim. 3, with reference to 1 Thess. 4.12.

'infidels' should be brought to the true faith 'by doctrine and example'.[233] In Grotius's view, the believers have a duty to contribute to the *voluntary* conversion of Jews, pagans and heretics to Christianity. Hence, those who are 'firm in their faith' are allowed to communicate with the non-believers, so that they may 'bring them to good sense'.[234] These considerations lead Grotius to formulate his third proposition: 'It is permissible to have some friendship and familiarity with non-believers and with heretics'.[235] According to Grotius, this is permissible, because it may contribute to their (voluntary) conversion to Christianity (or acceptance of the true Christian doctrine). However, it is permissible under the strict condition that contacts with non-believers and heretics do not cause the believers (e.g., those weak of faith) to fall away from the faith.

7.2.2 Private Alliances: Marriages Between Believers and Non-believers

After discussing the general conditions under which relations of friendship and familiarity with non-believers are permissible, Grotius turns to the more specific issue of marriage. In his fourth proposition, he addresses the question whether marriages between Christians and non-Christians can be lawful.[236] He begins by explaining that marriage is the 'highest union' (*summa coniunctio*); from a Christian perspective, it is considered a *sacred* bond, so that divorce is generally not allowed under the laws of the church.[237] However, mixed marriages between the believers and non-believers may also lead to apostasy if, for instance, a Christian wife is forced or induced to adopt the faith of her non-Christian husband. Grotius therefore distinguishes between marriages that have already been concluded and those that are still to be con-

233 The source is perhaps Vitoria's *De Indis*. Vitoria had argued that the war against the American Indians could not be justified by their lack of faith. Crucially, he believed that pagans and Jews could not be forced to convert to Christianity: threats and fear would only lead them to accept the true faith against their will, which was 'monstrous and sacrilegious'. He concluded that pagans and Jews could not be forced to convert to Christianity, but they could 'at least be forced to listen' to the Christian missionaries. If they refused to do so, then the war against them was justified. Vitoria, *De Indis*, q. 2, a. 3–4, § 36, concl. 3 and § 39, concl. 6.

234 In a similar vein, Grotius's draft regulations for the Jews included a provision (Art. 21) allowing 'Christian clergymen … to visit the congregation of the Jews, with the consent of the city government, to teach and preach to them about the Christian religion', and imposing a fine of a hundred guilders for anyone who refused to listen. Grotius, *Remonstrantie*, fol. 16^r, pp. 118–119, trans., p. 206.

235 Grotius, *De societate*, fol. 315^v, prop. 3.

236 Ibid., fol. 315^v, prop. 4.

237 See, e.g., Grat. *Decr.*, C. 32, q. 7, c. 2. The general prohibition of divorce was based on Math. 19.6: 'What God has joined together, let no one separate'.

cluded.[238] He argues that marriages that have already been concluded (e.g., *existing* marriages) are legally binding: thus, a Christian wife is not allowed to separate from her non-Christian husband, nor a Christian husband from his non-Christian wife.[239] This follows from 1 Cor. 7.12: 'If any brother hath a wife that believeth not, and she be pleased to dwell with him, let him not put her away'. However, it is permissible for a Christian magistrate to make a law declaring such existing marriages between believers and non-believers null and void. As Grotius explains, the magistrate may issue a law invalidating existing marriages if he has a 'just reason' for doing so. This follows from Ezra 10.3, which narrates how Ezra and the high priests of Israel swore an oath to send away the 'strange wives of the people of the land' to restore the covenant with God. Hence, according to Grotius, *existing* marriages between the believers and non-believers should in general be respected, and the believers are not allowed to separate from their infidel spouses, unless the magistrate has issued a law invalidating such marriages for a 'just reason'.

While *existing* marriages between the faithful and non-believers are generally binding, marriages that are still to be concluded (i.e., *future* marriages) should in general be prohibited. The reason is that, in Grotius's view, the main purpose of marriage is the upbringing of children to the glory of God, which is 'not a little hindered' if one of the parents is a non-believer.[240] To justify the general prohibition on future marriages between Christians and non-Christians, Grotius quotes 2 Cor. 6.14: 'Be you not unequally yoked together with unbelievers: for what fellowship hath righteousness with unrighteousness? And what communion hath light with darkness?' He adds a reference to Scaliger's *Animadversiones in Eusebium*, where it is suggested that Herodes was born from a mixed marriage, and that his (non-Jewish) mother had only been allowed to marry his Jewish father by accepting the Jewish rites. As Scaliger explains, while Moses and Nehemiah had prohibited marriages with Moabite women, in the

238 Grotius, *De societate*, fol. 315^{v}, prop. 4: 'Agitur autem aut de [matrimonio] contracto aut de contrahendo' ('Now it is a matter of either a concluded marriage or a marriage to be concluded'). See also Borschberg, 'De societate', p. 376.

239 Grotius, *De societate*, fol. 315^{v}, prop. 4: 'Contracto non licet ab Infideli divertere' ('In case of a concluded marriage it is not permissible to separate from the non-believer') and fol. 316 (1)^{r}, right column: 'Uxor a viro infideli divertere non debet' ('A wife should not divorce from an unfaithful husband'). Cf. De Wilde, 'Hugo Grotius's *De societate*', p. 434.

240 Grotius, *De societate*, fol. 315^{v}, prop. 5. For the same reason, Grotius, in his *Remonstrantie*, proposes that a 'child born from a Jewish father and a mother who has converted to the Christian religion or vice versa can be baptized at the request of the Christian father or mother, and being baptized, shall not be circumcised'. Grotius, *Remonstrantie*, fol. 18^{v}–19^{r}, pp. 128–131, trans., p. 207 (Art. 37).

course of time, marriages between Jewish men and pagan wives had become tacitly permitted, until, at the time of the Hasmoneans, it became a strict law that no Jew lived together with a pagan wife, not even secretly.[241] To justify the general prohibition on mixed marriages Grotius refers to the examples of Solomon, who had sinned by living together with pagan women, and Manasseh, brother of the high priest, who was said to have defiled the priesthood by such a marriage.[242] However, in accordance with Grotius's fifth premise, an exception should be made in cases of divine vocation. He refers to the example of Esther, who was 'perhaps' called to marry a non-believer, the Persian king Ahasuerus, so that she could reveal Haman's plot against the Jewish people.[243] In accordance with Grotius's fourth premise, an exception should also be made in cases of necessity, when the believers cannot conclude marriages, except with pagan women. This is the case when they find themselves in foreign places, where there are not enough marriage partners of their own faith.[244]

Grotius's discussion of marriages between the believers and non-believers in *De societate* seems to have informed his *Remonstrantie* or draft regulations for the Jews.[245] Thus, Article 27 of his regulations contains a general prohibition on marriages between Christians and Jews: no Jewish man shall be allowed to marry a Christian woman, nor a Jewish woman a Christian man.[246] To justify this prohibition Grotius cites the same biblical sources he had discussed in *De societate*.[247] He also suggests that the general prohibition on mixed marriages does not apply to marriages that have already been concluded. Thus, according to Article 36, if the wife of a Jewish husband has converted to Christianity, she will only obtain permission to separate from her husband and to live on her own if she is abused because of her faith.[248] In a note, Grotius explains that *existing* marriages between Jews and Christians should in general be respected: he refers to Paul's advice to the believers not to separate from their infidel spouses if they want to continue their cohabitation.[249] Invoking the example of

---

241 Scaliger, *Animadversiones in Chronologica Eusebii*, p. 149.
242 Neh. 13.26 and 28. In Grotius, *De societate*, fol. 315^{v}, prop. 5.
243 See the reference to Esther in Grotius, *De societate*, fol. 315^{v}, prop. 5, lim.
244 Ibid., fol. 315^{v}, prop. 5, lim. Cf. *IBP*, II.2.21, where it is argued that foreigners have a right to marry local women if they lack their own marriage partners, 'as, for example, in case a large number of men has been expelled from one place and has come to another'.
245 Borschberg, 'De societate', p. 376 and De Wilde, 'Hugo Grotius's *De Societate*', pp. 434–435.
246 Grotius, *Remonstrantie*, fol. 17^{r}, pp. 122–123, trans., p. 207 (Art. 27).
247 Neh. 13.26 and 28. The *Remonstrance* mentions two additional sources: Deut. 7.7 and 1 Reg. 11. See Grotius, *Remonstrantie*, fol. 26 [=27]^{v}, pp. 164–165, trans., p. 212 (sub Art. 27).
248 Grotius, *Remonstrantie*, fol. 18^{v}, pp. 128–129, trans., p. 207 (Art. 36).
249 Ibid., fol. 28 [=29]^{v}, pp. 172–173, trans., p. 213 (sub Art. 36).

Ezra, he argues that the magistrate may prohibit such marriages by public order for a special reason, for instance, if one of the spouses abuses the other in regard of religion.[250] Hence, in his *Remonstrantie*, Grotius applies the same distinctions he had developed in *De societate*: marriages between Christians and Jews that are still to be concluded (i.e., *future* marriages) are generally forbidden. However, marriages that have already been concluded (i.e., *existing* marriages) should in general be respected, and the magistrate may only invalidate such marriages for a just reason. Moreover, he refers to the same biblical sources (e.g., 1 Cor. 7.12 and Ezra 10) to justify these distinctions.[251]

7.2.3 Public Alliances: Treaties of Friendship and Military Alliances

After discussing the issue of mixed marriages as an example of 'private alliances', Grotius turns to the question of 'public alliances'. Building on his second proposition that the believers should do good to non-believers and heretics, he formulates his second conclusion: '[t]reaties with the non-believers are rightly entered into for the sake of friendship, commerce, travels, and other benefits which are mutually guaranteed'.[252] Grotius mentions the example of Solomon's treaty with Hiram, which entailed 'peace and alliance' (*pax et foedus*) and 'trade' (*commercium*).[253] However, as Grotius realizes, the Bible also contains several passages that seem to condemn the believers for entering into treaties and alliances with non-believers. Grotius refers to 2 Chr. 20.37, where Josephat's treaty with Ahaziah is identified as the cause of divine wrath.[254] Recalling his sixth premise, Grotius explains that this treaty was not unlawful in itself, but condemned because of Ahaziah's 'wicked' intentions.[255] He suggests that there may 'perhaps' have been a special reason for condemning the treaty, as the king of Israel was an apostate.[256] The implication is that, as a general rule, it is permissible for the faithful to enter into treaties of friendship or trade with non-believers, unless such treaties should be condemned for a 'special reason'

250 Ibid., fol. 28 [=29]^{v} and 29 [=30]^{r}, pp. 172–175, trans., p. 213 (sub Art. 36).

251 Apart from the references to 1 Cor. 7.12 and Ezra 10, Grotius also refers to the example of the Moabite women to justify a prohibition on sexual relations between Jews and Christians: 'It is found in the Talmud that a law was established during the rule of the Hasmoneans pertaining to unlawful sexual intercourse with a pagan woman'. Ibid., fol. 30 [=31]^{r}, pp. 178–179, trans., p. 214 (sub Art. 38).

252 Grotius, *De societate*, fol. 317^{r}.

253 1 Reg. 5.12 (according to the verse numbering of the Vulgate), in ibid., fol. 316 (1)^{r}, left column.

254 See also the reading notes, ibid., fol. 316 (1)^{r}.

255 2 Chr. 20.35–36.

256 Grotius, *De societate*, fol. 317^{r}.

or because of the 'inner state of mind' of the contracting parties. Moreover, the general rule that it is permissible for the believers to enter into treaties of trade or friendship with non-believers is subject to an important condition: the believers should receive greater, not lesser, benefits from those treaties than the non-believers.[257]

Apart from treaties of friendship and trade, the believers may also enter into *military* alliances with non-believers.[258] Grotius recalls his eighth premise, in which he had made a distinction between defensive and offensive alliances (ἐπιμαχία and συμμαχία).[259] In his reading notes, he presents a sub-distinction between the various types of defensive and offensive alliances which can be concluded between the believers and non-believers. In case of defensive alliances, they can either be alliances for the defense of the believers, or for the defense of the non-believers. In case of offensive alliances, they can either be aimed against the believers, or against the non-believers.[260] In accordance with his tenth premise, Grotius explains that a military alliance—whether defensive or offensive—may not be entered into for every future war without exception. Instead, for such an alliance to be justified, there should be a *justa causa belli*.[261] In *De societate*, Grotius does not explain what causes of war are justified. However, in *De iure praedae*, he had specified that a just war could be waged on four grounds: self-defense, the defense of one's property, the enforcement of rights arising out of debt, and punishment for wrongdoing.[262] The fourth ground implied that a just war could be waged not only to protect one's own rights, but also to protect the rights of others and, more particularly, 'to defend the victims of unjust oppression'.[263] As we will see below, in *De societate*, Grotius mentions both self-defense and the defense of the victims of unjust oppression as possible justifications for military alliances with non-believers.

The question whether military alliances with non-believers could be lawful and legitimate had been the topic of a centuries-old debate among jurists and

257 Ibid., fol. 317^{r}, restr.

258 Ibid., fol. 317^{r}, in prem.

259 Ibid., fol. 317^{r}, in prem.

260 Ibid., fol. 316 (2)^{v}, left column: 'Societas ad def[ensionem] fidelis; vel ad defensionem infidelis; vel ad off[ensionem]. Item contra fid[eles] aut contra infid[eles]'.

261 Ibid., fol. 317^{r}, in prem.

262 *IPC*, ed. Hamaker, pp. 67–68, ed. Van Ittersum, pp. 102–103. Cf. *IBP*, prol. 8, where Grotius distinguishes five rather than four just grounds for war, by splitting obligations from debt into obligations out of contract and out of delict. See Lesaffer, 'The Laws of War- and Peace-Making', p. 446 and Haggenmacher, *Grotius et la doctrine de la guerre juste*, pp. 176 ff.

263 Cf. *IPC*, ed. Hamaker, p. 60, ed. Van Ittersum, p. 93.

theologians.[264] As Tuck explains, the main question was whether it was permissible for Christians to use the assistance of non-believers in a war against other Christians.[265] Medieval canonists had concluded that military alliances with non-believers had to be condemned, especially if they were aimed against Christians. According to the ordinary gloss to the Decretals, 'Christians who attack other Christians in alliance with Saracens, either by supplying help or by participating themselves, are worse than Saracens. By canon law they are condemned to slavery and can be repeatedly excommunicated'.[266] More positive attitudes towards military alliances with non-Christians had started to emerge in the fourteenth century, as the papacy decided to support Charles of Anjou, who used the assistance of Moslems in his attempts to conquer Southern Italy.[267] For instance, in his *Consilia*, Oldradus de Ponte, a jurist at the papal court at Avignon, argued that it was sometimes permissible for Christians to enter into alliances with non-Christians to defend their own lives and possessions. However, Oldradus did not discuss alliances that were aimed against Christians.[268] By contrast, John of Naples, a Dominican theologian, claimed that, in cases of 'urgent necessity', a Christian ruler could use the aid of non-believers, even against other Christians.[269] In his reading notes, Grotius briefly refers to Oldradus's views on military alliances with non-believers, but he does not mention John of Naples.[270]

By the beginning of the sixteenth century, the predominant view had become that military alliances with non-believers could be legitimate, but only if they were *defensive* alliances.[271] This view was expressed in the *Summa Sylves-*

264 On these debates see Tuck, 'Alliances with Infidels', pp. 61–83 and Condorelli, 'Grotius's Doctrine of Alliances with Infidels', pp. 17–24.

265 Tuck, 'Alliances with Infidels', p. 63.

266 Gloss (*casus*) to the Decretals 5.6.6 *Ita quorundam*, in *Decretales D. Gregorii Papae IX una cum glossis restitutae* (Roma: In aedibus populi Romani, 1582), col. 1658. Trans. in Tuck, 'Alliances with Infidels', p. 63.

267 Tuck, 'Alliances with Infidels', p. 64.

268 Oldradus de Ponte, *Consilia* (Venetiis: Apud Franciscum Zilettum, 1570), fol. 27 (cons. 71).

269 Arthur McGrade, John Kilcullen and Matthew Kempshall (ed.), *The Cambridge Translations of Medieval Philosophical Texts* (Cambridge: Cambridge University Press, 2011), 2, p. 346, quoted in Tuck, 'Alliances with Infidels', p. 65.

270 Grotius refers to Oldradus de Ponte, *Consilia*, cons. 67. However, the relevant text can be found in cons. 71: 'Bellum si sit iustum Christianus potest sine peccato ad defensionem suam uti auxilio infidelium pro parte sua' (Oldradus, *Consilia*, 71 (27)). Grotius may have taken the reference to 'Oldr. cons. 67' from *Abbatis Panormitani … in tertium Decretalium librum commentaria* (Venetiis: Bernardus Maiorinus, 1569), fol. 223^{v}. Cf. the reference to Oldradus, cons. 71 in *IBP*, II.15.8 (ed. Feenstra, p. 395, n. 5).

271 Marc de Wilde, 'Protecting Non-Christian Allies: Hugo Grotius's Justification of Dutch Overseas Expansion', in *Avant l'état: Droit international et pluralisme politico-juridique en*

trina of the Dominican theologian Silvester Mazzolini da Prierio, and quoted by Grotius in his reading notes: 'Christians having a just war for their own defense can use peaceful infidels who have no active or passive war with us; when necessity is pressing, not otherwise'.[272] As Sylvester explained, using the aid of non-Christians was allowed for purposes of self-defense, provided that the 'infidels' were not themselves at war with Christians, and only in cases of 'imminent necessity'. Sylvester had referred to the opinion of Nicholas of Lyra, a fourteenth-century Franciscan theologian—a reference which Grotius also included in his reading notes.[273] Nicholas had given the example of David, who had justly used the military aid of the Philistines against his own people, because he had a right to the kingship of Israel.[274] In his reading notes (just below the references to Nicholas and Sylvester), Grotius also mentions two contemporary examples, of kings 'Francis' and 'Antoine'.[275] Unfortunately, he does not elaborate on these examples, and it remains uncertain which kings or alliances he has in mind. Grotius may have thought of the military alliance between Francis I of France and Suleiman the Magnificent of the Ottoman Empire (1536), which was aimed against the Habsburg emperor.[276] By referring to the opinions of Nicholas and Sylvester, the example of David's alliance with the Philistines, and (perhaps) France's alliance with the Ottomans, Grotius suggests that alliances with non-believers are permissible in cases of self-defense, even if they are aimed against other Christians.

While medieval jurists and theologians had accepted alliances with non-believers only in cases of 'urgent necessity' and 'self-defense', the sixteenth-century Iberian jurists were less reluctant to accept such alliances, because they recognized their importance for empire-building in Asia and the Americas.[277] For instance, in his lecture on the American 'Indians', Vitoria had argued that the Spaniards could wage a just war on behalf of non-Christian allies, even if they were not themselves attacked. As Vitoria explained, the Spaniards

---

Europe, XIIIe–XVIIe siècle, ed. by Dante Fedele, Randall Lesaffer and Pierre Savy (Rome: Historia et ius, 2024), pp. 269–289.

272 Sylvester, *Sylvestrinae Summae*, I, 93 (left column), on 'Bellum I' ('De bello publico'), 8, concl. 3. Grotius, *De societate*, fol. 316 (2)^v, left column.

273 The opinion of Nicholas is discussed just before that of John of Naples in ibid., 93 (right column), on 'Bellum I' ('De bello publico'), 8, concl. 3.

274 1 Sam. 28.

275 Perhaps a reference to Francis I (1494–1547) or Francis II (1544–1560), kings of France, and Antoine (1518–1562), king of Navarra, father of Henry IV. In Grotius, *De societate*, fol. 316 (2)^v, left column.

276 Cf. Tuck, 'Alliances with Infidels', p. 66.

277 Ibid., p. 67.

had a *justa causa belli* if their (non-Christian) allies were engaged in a just war among themselves and had requested their assistance.[278] However, Vitoria referred to Spain's alliance with the Tlaxcaltecs against the Aztecs, and he did not discuss alliances that were aimed against Christians.[279] Other Spanish jurists, such as Luis de Molina and Francisco de Suarez, accepted the legitimacy of alliances with non-believers, but they also warned that such alliances could lead to a scandal for Christianity if they were aimed against Christians.[280] By contrast, Protestant jurists generally rejected alliances with 'infidels', irrespective of whether they were aimed against Christians or non-Christians. By the end of the sixteenth-century, the standard Protestant view had become that no military alliances with non-Christians were permitted at all.[281] This view was expressed by Alberico Gentili, who concluded that 'it is lawful neither to lend aid to unbelievers nor to accept aid from them against other unbelievers. And if it is not lawful to do this against unbelievers, how much less will it be allowed to do it against the faithful?'[282]

The reading notes of *De societate* contain several references to Vitoria and Gentili.[283] Strikingly, Grotius does not refer to Gentili's chapter on alliances with non-believers (in which military alliances with non-believers are expressly rejected), but to another chapter, entitled 'On Defending the Subjects of Another Against their Sovereign [*De subditis alienis contra Dominum defendis*]'.[284] In this chapter, Gentili explains that it is sometimes just to defend the subjects of another sovereign if a 'dispute [arises] regarding the state [*controversia de re publica*]' and if they are treated 'cruelly and unjustly [*inclementer et injuste*]'.[285] Aiding the subjects of another sovereign is permissible even if one's own cause is unjust, but only with the purpose of saving them from 'immoderate cruelty and unmerciful punishment [*saevitiae immoderatioris, & poenae*

278 Vitoria, *De Indis*, q. 3, a. 7, § 17.

279 Ibid., q. 3, a. 7, § 17.

280 Luis de Molina, *De iustitia* (Venetiis: Apud minimam societatem, 1594), disp. 112, 463–464; Francisco Suarez, *Selections from Three Works of Francisco Suarez*, trans. Gwladys L. Williams, Ammi Brown and John Waldron (Oxford: Clarendon Press, 1944), vol. 2, p. 853; Tuck, 'Alliances with Infidels', p. 67.

281 Tuck, 'Alliances with Infidels', p. 68.

282 Alberico Gentili, *De iure belli libri tres*, photographic reproduction and English translation of the 1612 edition, trans. by John C. Rolfe and introd. by Coleman Phillipson (Oxford: Clarendon, 1933), book III, chapter 19 (Latin original, p. 659; English translation, p. 402). Quoted in Tuck, 'Alliances with Infidels', p. 69.

283 Grotius, *De societate*, fol. 316 (2)^{v}, left column (Vitoria) and right column (Gentili).

284 Gentili, *De iure belli*, I.16 (Latin orig., pp. 118–127; English trans., pp. 74–78).

285 Ibid., I.16 (Latin orig., p. 120; English trans., p. 75).

inclementioris]'.[286] By referring to these passages in the context of a discussion of military alliances with non-believers, Grotius implies that such alliances may be legitimate if they serve to protect the non-believers from inhumane treatment. Crucially, for Grotius, military alliances with non-Christians are justified not only in cases of self-defense, but also for defending the non-believers from unjust oppression. Ignoring Gentili's objections against military alliances with non-Christians, Grotius suggests that Gentili's arguments regarding the legitimate defense of the subjects of another sovereign may also apply to non-Christians: hence, military alliances with non-Christians can be just if they serve to protect the 'infidels' from oppression.[287]

Even more revealing are Grotius's references to Vitoria. In his reading notes, Grotius refers twice to passages in *De Indis*, in which Vitoria discussed the various just titles by which the American 'Indians' had passed under the rule of the Spaniards. Grotius refers to the fifth just title: the defense of the innocent against tyranny.[288] As Vitoria argued, the Spaniards could wage a just war to protect the subjects of Indian rulers against tyranny and inhumane practices such as human sacrifice and cannibalism.[289] Referring to these passages, Grotius explains that Christians may enter into an 'alliance for the defense of some of the non-believers against the non-believers' (*societas pro defensione singulorum infid*[*elium*] *contra infid*[*eles*]).[290] In the reading notes, he also mentions Vitoria's seventh just title: the assistance of (non-Christian) allies.[291] Vitoria had argued that the Spaniards could wage a just war against the Indians 'whenever the barbarians are engaged in a legitimate war with one another, in

286 Ibid., I.16 (Latin orig., p. 123; English trans., p. 76).

287 The reading notes of *De societate* also contain a brief reference to Gentili's discussion 'of rebels and traitors [*De rebellibus et proditoribus*]' (fol. 316 (2)^{v}, right column). It is perhaps a reference to Gentili's argument in book III that rebellion is itself the chief incentive to cruelty, so that rebels and traitors may be treated more severely than common enemies (Gentili, *De iure belli*, III.7, p. 521, trans., p. 320). However, as a separate chapter with this title is lacking, it may also be a reference to the chapter mentioned above, where Gentili explains that the English had justly provided military assistance to the Dutch against the Spaniards (ibid., I.16, p. 124, trans., p. 77). Of course, the war between Spain and the Dutch Republic originated from a religious dispute (among other causes), so that from the Spanish perspective, the English had aided 'heretics'. Needless to say, it is unlikely that Gentili's defense of the Anglo-Dutch alliance escaped Grotius's attention.

288 Grotius, *De societate*, fol. 316 (2)^{v}, left column.

289 Vitoria, *De Indis*, q. 3, a. 5, § 15.

290 Grotius, *De societate*, fol. 316 (2)^{v}, left column.

291 Vitoria, *De Indis*, q. 3, a. 7, § 17: 'titulus societatis & amicitiae'. The reference can be found in ibid., fol. 316 (2)^{v}, left column.

which case the injured party has the right to wage war, and may call upon the Spaniards to help them, and then share the prizes of victory with them'.[292] As we have seen, Vitoria had given the example of the Spanish alliance with the Tlaxcaltecs, who were fighting a war against the Aztecs. As Vitoria explained, the Spaniards had made a treaty with the Tlaxcaltecs that they would help them to defeat the Aztecs and receive in return whatever booty they might seize.[293] In his reading notes, Grotius refers to this passage, explaining that it relates to an 'alliance with a non-believer who is waging a just war against a non-believer who is waging an unjust war' (*societas cum infideli iuste bellante contra inf[idelem] iniuste bellantem*).[294] On Grotius's reading of Vitoria, the believers may thus enter into military alliances with non-believers, provided that their allies are waging a just war against other non-believers.

The references to Vitoria appear to be the main source for Grotius's third conclusion: '[I]n a just war the non-believers will be rightly defended by the faithful, even if those who oppress the non-believers wish to be considered as faithful [*etiamsi ii qui Infideles opprimunt Fideles haberi velint*]. Nay, this work is not only permitted, but also highly praiseworthy, and because of the circumstances often necessary'.[295] Like Vitoria, Grotius maintains that a war may be waged to defend the non-believers from inhumane cruelty and oppression. However, in sharp contrast to Vitoria, he argues that the non-believers may rightly be defended even if those who oppress them 'wish to be considered as faithful'. Had Vitoria referred to military alliances between Christians (e.g., the Spaniards) and non-Christians (e.g., the Tlaxaltecs) that were aimed against non-Christians (e.g., the Aztecs), Grotius concludes that alliances for defending non-Christians from oppression may even be directed against Christians. As we have seen, Grotius's conclusion was probably meant to justify the Dutch alliances with non-Christian rulers in the East Indies, which were aimed against the Spaniards and Portuguese.[296] Thus, in *De iure praedae*, Grotius had used similar arguments to justify the Dutch alliance with the Sultan of Johor, which, in his view, served to defend the Sultan and his people from Iberian 'oppression'. As Grotius explained, 'not only is it universally admitted that the protection of infidels from injury (even from injury by Christians) is never unjust, but it is furthermore maintained, by authorities who have examined this particular point, that alliances and treaties with infidels may in many cases be justly

292 Vitoria, *De Indis*, q. 3, a. 7, § 17.

293 Ibid., q. 3, a. 7, § 17.

294 Grotius, *De societate*, fol. 316 (2)^v, left column.

295 Ibid., fol. 317^r, concl. 3.

296 Borschberg, 'De societate', p. 389; De Wilde, 'Hugo Grotius's *De societate*', pp. 430 and 432.

contracted for the purpose of defending one's own rights, too'.[297] As Grotius concluded, it was permissible for Christians to enter into military alliances with non-Christians, even if they were aimed against other Christians. Such alliances were justified not only to protect the rights of the believers themselves (e.g., to free navigation and trade), but also the rights of their 'infidel' allies (e.g., not to be oppressed).

As Grotius explains in his third conclusion, protecting the non-believers from oppression is not only praiseworthy, but it may even be necessary.[298] As Grotius indicates, this follows from the amplification of his second proposition: the believers have a duty to lend assistance to non-believers, if they can do so without great disadvantage for themselves, and especially if the non-believers have requested their assistance. To prove the conclusion that in these circumstances, Christians have a duty to protect non-Christians from oppression, Grotius refers to Psalm 82.4: 'Deliver the poor and needy: rid them out of the hand of the wicked', and Prov. 24.11: 'Deliver them that are drawn unto death, and forebear not to deliver those that are ready to be slain'. By citing these biblical verses Grotius implies that the duty to protect the innocent from unjust oppression originates from divine law itself. In *De Indis*, Vitoria had also referred to Prov. 24.11 to demonstrate that the Spaniards could wage a just war to prevent 'Indian' rulers from subjecting their own people to inhumane customs and rites.[299] By contrast, Grotius cites Prov. 24.11 and Psalm 82.4 to conclude that, depending on the circumstances, Christians have a duty to protect the non-believers from unjust oppression, even if those who oppress them are Christians. However, an exception should be made if it has been revealed that God wants to punish particular nations for their unbelief. The believers are thus prohibited from entering into military alliances with nations that have been condemned by God (irrespective of whether or not they are unjustly oppressed).[300]

---

297 *IPC*, ed. Hamaker, p. 298, ed. Van Ittersum, p. 434. The authorities to whom Grotius referred in this passage included Panormitanus and Vitoria: Panormitanus, gloss to *c. quod super de voto*, *In tertium Decretalium librum commentaria* (Venetiis: Bernardus Maiorinus, 1569), fol. 223^{v}–224^{r} (*Decretal.*, 3.34.8) and Vitoria, *De Indis*, q. 3, a. 5, §15 and a. 7, §17. Grotius also added a reference to Franciscus Arias, *De bello et eius iustitia*, in *Tractatus illustrium … iurisconsultorum* (Venetiis, 1584), tom. XVI, fol. 325^{r}–335^{r}, no. 192 (on fol. 334^{r}).

298 Grotius, *De societate*, fol. 317^{r}, concl. 3.

299 As Vitoria explained, the duty to save the oppressed 'applies not only to the actual moment when they are being dragged to death; they [the Spaniards] may also force the barbarians to give up such rites altogether. If they refuse to do so, war may be declared upon them'. In Vitoria, *De Indis*, q. 3, a. 5, §15.

300 Grotius, *De societate*, fol. 317^{r}, concl. 3, lim.

According to Grotius's fourth conclusion, the believers may also themselves request the military assistance of non-believers, provided that they have a just cause for war.[301] In his reading notes, Grotius mentions several sources to justify this conclusion, including Panormitanus's gloss on the Decretals, which expressly states that 'it is lawful for Christians to use the assistance of infidels',[302] and the advice of Oldradus that 'if a war is just, a Christian may without sin use, for his own defense, the aid of infidels on his part'.[303] The reading notes also mention several biblical examples of wars waged by the believers with the military assistance of non-believers, for instance, the war of the Israelites against Nebuchadnezzar, for which they had requested the assistance of the king of Egypt.[304] However, unlike Panormitanus and Oldradus, Grotius suggests that the believers may use the military assistance of non-believers for any just cause whatsoever, not only for self-defense, but also for protecting others from oppression. Moreover, he explains that military assistance of non-believers should be regarded as a 'benefit' (*beneficium*). He refers to a passage from Seneca's *De beneficiis*, where it is argued that one should accept benefits only from those to whom one could have given such benefits, that is, from honorable men.[305] As Seneca explains, this does not exclude the possibility that in cases of necessity, a benefit may also be received from dishonorable men, such as tyrants, pirates or brigands, 'for necessity removes any possibility of choice'.[306] In other words: in a just war, the believers may accept the assistance of non-believers, just as benefits may be received from dishonorable men in cases of necessity.

However, Grotius's conclusion that the believers may wage a just war with the assistance of non-believers is made subject to two conditions. The first is that using the assistance of non-believers is not permitted if it gives them an 'occasion for harming the truth' (*occasio nocendi veritati*).[307] This condition follows from the second premise that the believers should carefully guard against anything that may harm the true religion: hence, using the military assistance

301 Ibid., fol. 317^r, concl. 4.

302 Panormitanus, gloss on *Decretal.*, 3.34.8 *c. quod super de voto*, fol. 223^v–224^r. In Grotius, *De societate*, fol. 316 (2)^v, left column. Cf. the references to Panormitanus in *c. quod super de voto* in *IPC*, ed. Hamaker, p. 298, n. 3, ed. Van Ittersum, p. 434, n. d., and *IBP* II.15.10.4. (ed. Feenstra, p. 401, n. 1).

303 Oldradus, *Consilia*, 67 (=71) (fol. 223^v). Cf. the reference to Oldradus, cons. 71 in *IBP*, II.15.8 (ed. Feenstra, 395, n. 5).

304 Jes. 31.1 and 36.6, in Grotius, *De societate*, fol. 316 (2)^v, left column.

305 See the reference to Sen. *ben.* 2.18, in Grotius, *De societate*, fol. 317^r, concl. 4.

306 Sen. *ben.* 2.18.

307 Grotius, *De societate*, fol. 317^r, concl. 4, sub 1.

of non-believers is not allowed if it undermines the authority of God or hinders the spread of the Gospel. The second condition is that, even in a just war, the assistance of non-believers may not be used if it is done out of 'distrust' (*diffidentia*).[308] There are different ways to interpret this condition. The first is that the believers, in accepting the assistance of non-believers, may not themselves be driven by a lack of faith. In his reading notes, Grotius gives the example of Asa, King of Judah, who had entered into an alliance with Syria, because he had lost faith in God.[309] The second interpretation is that, in any war, both the believers and the non-believers remain bound by the requirements of good faith or 'public trust' (*fides publica*). This requires them, among other things, to show moderation in exercising power or coercion, even if doing so is permitted by the laws of war. In an early treatise, entitled *De fide et perfidia* (*Of Good and Bad Faith*, ca. 1601–1602), Grotius had argued that the requirements of public trust originated from natural law, i.e., from the natural fellowship between men.[310] Therefore, they applied irrespective of religious differences.[311] As Grotius would later put it in *De iure belli ac pacis*, 'no war ought to be so much undertaken but for the obtaining of a right, nor when undertaken, ought to be carried beyond the bounds of Justice and Fidelity'.[312] In Grotius's view, it was thus permissible for Christians to use the assistance of non-believers in war, provided that the believers did not violate the obligations of 'public trust'.

7.2.4 Unequal Alliances: The State and Slavery

In the final part of *De societate*, Grotius addresses the question of intra-state relations between the believers and non-believers. According to his fifth conclusion, 'the highest public partnership is the union of the state [*unio reipub-*

308 Ibid., 317ʳ, concl. 4, sub 2.

309 Ibid., fol. 316 (1)ʳ, left column. Cf. *IBP* II.15.9.9.

310 Hugo Grotius, 'De fide et perfidia' (Latin text and English translation), trans. and introd. by Arthur Eyffinger, *Grotiana*, 36 (2015), 79–171. See also Wolfgang Fikentscher, *De Fide et Perfidia: Der Treuegedanke in den Staatsparallelen des Hugo Grotius aus heutiger Sicht* (Munich: Verlag der Bayerischen Akademie der Wissenschaften, 1979); Hans Blom, 'The Meaning of Trust: *Fides* between Self-Interest and *Appetitus Societatis*', in *The Roots of International Law/ Les fondements du droit international: Liber Amicorum Peter Haggenmacher*, ed. by Pierre-Marie Dupuy and Vincent Chetail (Leiden: Brill, 2014), pp. 39–58; Hans Blom, 'Hugo Grotius on Trust: Its Causes and Effects', in *Trust and Happiness in the History of Political Thought*, ed. by László Kontler and Mark Somos (Leiden: Brill, 2018), pp. 76–98; Peter Schröder, 'Trust (*fides*)', in *The Cambridge Companion to Hugo Grotius*, pp. 118–137; Marc de Wilde, '*Fides publica* in Ancient Rome and its Reception by Grotius and Locke', *Tijdschrift voor rechtsgeschiedenis*, 79 (2011), 455–487.

311 De Wilde, '*Fides publica*', p. 467.

312 Grotius, *De iure belli ac pacis*, prol. 26.

licae]. But there is no doubt that a faithful people can remain in one state with non-believers'.[313] As we have seen, both Cicero and Aquinas had characterized the state (*res publica*) as a *societas publica*.[314] They had defined the state as an assemblage of people who, in Cicero's words, had 'associated [*sociatus*] in an agreement with respect to justice and a partnership for the common good'.[315] As Cicero explained in *De re publica*, this association originated not so much from the weakness of individuals, but from a 'certain natural fellowship of men'.[316] Building on Cicero's understanding of the state as an 'association' originating from nature itself, Grotius concludes that it can encompass both the believers and non-believers. According to Grotius, the believers can therefore live together in one state with non-believers and even with heretics. To justify this conclusion Grotius refers to Scaliger, who, in his *Animadversiones in Eusebium*, had discussed the example of the Jews, who had lived together in one state with the Idumaeans (or Edomites).[317] He also mentions the example of 'Israel with Egypt', perhaps a reference to the fact that the Israelites had settled in Egypt after one of them, Joseph, had become a high official at the court of Pharaoh.[318] As Grotius suggests, the believers may live together in one state with non-believers, because as the 'highest public partnership', the state originates from the natural community of mankind, which includes both the faithful and non-believers.

However, according to Grotius's sixth conclusion, it is doubtful whether the believers may *voluntarily* join a state with non-believers.[319] Grotius draws a parallel with his discussion of marriage: just as the purpose of marriage is to educate children 'to the glory of God', the end of a 'true state' is to direct its citizens to divine glory, which may be hindered if the state is shared with non-believers. Living together in one state with non-believers may thus lead to apostasy if a Christian subject is forced or induced by a non-Christian government to give up his faith, just as a Christian wife may be induced or forced to adopt the religion of her non-Christian husband. To prevent these risks, Grotius indicates that the 'same thing should be taught' (*idem docendum*) in regard of the state as was taught in regard of marriage: if the believers are *already* living together in one state with non-believers, then they may continue to do so. However,

313 Grotius, *De societate*, fol. 317^{r}, concl. 5.

314 Cic. *rep.* 1.25.39; Aquinas, *Liber contra impugnantes Dei cultum et religionem*, pars 2, c. 2, corp.

315 Cf. Cic. *rep.* 1.25.39 (trans. Clinton Walker Keyes).

316 Cic. *rep.* 1.25.39: 'naturalis quaedam hominum quasi congregatio' (trans. modified).

317 Scaliger, *Animadversiones in Chronologica Eusebii*, p. 148.

318 Gen. 41.40 and 46.6.

319 Grotius, *De societate*, fol. 317^{r}, concl. 6.

the believers should not be allowed to *start* living together with non-believers, unless a necessity requires them to do so. Grotius does not give an example, but one could think of the situation in which non-Christians (e.g., Jews) have been driven from their homes and can find a refuge only in a Christian state.[320] Moreover, as Grotius emphasizes, the conclusion that the believers should not 'voluntarily' (*sponte*) live together in one state with non-believers applies especially to those 'who have departed from the church'.[321] In other words, in an ideal situation, no state should be shared with heretics or apostates. However, in existing states, the believers are often already living together with heretics and apostates, which in itself should not be considered a violation of Christian law, especially if the latter are encouraged to return to the true religion.

Grotius's conclusion in *De societate* that a faithful people may live together in one state with non-believers (albeit not voluntarily) may have informed his later arguments regarding the admittance of Jews to Holland and West-Friesland. In his *Remonstrantie*, Grotius begins by presenting several reasons for a Christian government *not* to admit religious minorities such as Jews. Most importantly, as Grotius observes, 'religious unity is the greatest strength of a powerful state', and it is therefore 'not advisable to receive people in a country whose religion differs so much from ours'.[322] The greatest risk is that the presence of Jews will 'instill doubt in the weak-minded regarding the principal points that are necessary for our salvation'.[323] In other words, admitting the Jews may increase religious division in a Christian state and lead to apostasy if their presence causes the 'weak-minded' to turn away from the true faith. However, as Grotius explains, there are also 'excellent arguments' for admitting the Jews, which 'perhaps ought to take priority over the previous ones'.[324] Most importantly, the believers have a duty to contribute to the (voluntary) conversion of the Jews, 'which will not come about if the Jews are forbidden to live among Christians'.[325] In Grotius's view, the Jews should preferably live among *Reformed* Christians, who have turned away from (Catholic) idolatry and iconolatry; otherwise, their conversion to Christianity cannot be expected (especially since the Jews themselves reject the Catholic worship of statues). Apart from these religious arguments, Grotius gives another, more principled reason for admitting the Jews: referring to Justinian's *Digest*, he observes that

320 Cf. *IBP*, II.2.16 and Grotius, *Remonstrantie*, fol. 8^{v}, pp. 88–89, trans., p. 203.
321 *De societate*, fol. 317^{r}, concl. 6.
322 Grotius, *Remonstrantie*, fol. 2^{r}, pp. 62–63, trans., p. 199.
323 Ibid., fol. 2^{r}, pp. 62–63, trans., p. 199.
324 Ibid., fol. 5^{r}, pp. 74–75, trans., p. 202.
325 Ibid., fol. 5^{v}, pp. 76–77, trans., p. 202.

'nature has established a kind of kinship between all people'.[326] From this natural kinship follows a duty for all nations to receive strangers and to treat them well.[327] As this duty originates from natural law, it applies independently of religion: hence, the States of Holland and West-Friesland have a duty to provide hospitality to the Jews, irrespective of their religious 'errors'.

For Grotius, the state is an example of an unequal *public* society, as citizens are subject to the authority and jurisdiction of their government. By contrast, the relationship between servants or slaves and their masters is an example of an unequal *private* society, as slaves or servants are dependent on their masters, whose commands they are required to obey. As Grotius explains in *De societate*, in unequal societies such as these, the faithful can either be the superior or the inferior party. Whether the believers are allowed to join *unequal* societies with non-believers generally depends on whether it contributes to the spread of the Gospel, or, conversely, entails the risk of apostasy. Hence, Grotius's sixth proposition is that '[i]t is permissible for the faithful to have non-believers as servants and even as slaves'.[328] As evidence Grotius refers to a passage in Aquinas's *Summa theologiae*, where it is stated that 'Christians can have unbelievers, either Jews, or pagans, or Saracens, for servants'.[329] Aquinas gives the following reason: 'There is more probability that a servant who is ruled by his master's commands, will be converted to the faith of his master who is a believer, than if the case were reverse: and so the faithful are not forbidden to have unbelieving servants'.[330] The believers may thus have non-believers as their servants or slaves, because it contributes to their conversion to Christianity. However, Aquinas makes an exception for situations in which the master, by communicating with his infidel servant or slave, may himself be persuaded to give up the Christian faith. In those cases, the master should send his infidel servant or slave away, to prevent the risk of apostasy.[331]

In the propositions and conclusions that follow, Grotius draws a parallel between the state as an unequal *public* society and the master-slave relationship as an unequal *private* society.[332] Just as the believers may generally have non-believers as their servants or slaves, a Christian government may in gen-

326 *Dig.* 1.1.3, quoted in ibid., fol. 6[r], pp. 78–79, trans., p. 202.

327 Ibid., fol. 6[v], pp. 80–81, trans., p. 202. Cf. De Wilde, 'Offering Hospitality to Strangers', pp. 410–411.

328 Grotius, *De societate*, fol. 317[r], prop. 6.

329 *S. Th.* 2 2ae, q. 10, a. 9.

330 *S. Th.* 2 2ae, q. 10, a. 9, resp. ad 3.

331 *S. Th.* 2 2ae, q. 10, a. 9, resp. ad 3.

332 Cf. *IBP*, 1.4.4, where it is observed that the same principles underlying the duty of slaves to obey their masters apply to the duty of subjects to obey their kings.

eral accept non-Christians as its subjects. Grotius's seventh conclusion is that it is 'equally permissible for a faithful magistrate or people to accept an infidel people under its authority'.[333] The same reason applies to the state as applies to the master-slave relationship: there is more probability that non-Christians will convert to Christianity if they are subject to a Christian government than if the case were reverse, for, as subjects of a Christian government, they will be inclined to adopt the faith of their rulers. Hence, a Christian magistrate or people may in general accept an infidel people under its authority, unless it entails the risk of apostasy. Here Grotius formulates the general principles that he will later, in his *Remonstrantie*, use as arguments for admitting Jews to the Dutch provinces. As we have seen, the 'principal reason' for admitting the Jews is that it will contribute to their (voluntary) conversion to Christianity.[334] As the Jews become subject to a Christian government, it is more likely that they will convert to Christianity, especially if they are allowed to live among Reformed Christians, who have rejected Catholic idolatry and worship of statues.

These passages in *De societate* show that unequal societies between the believers and non-believers—whether the state as an unequal 'public society' or the master-slave relationship as an unequal 'private society'—are allowed only if the believers are the superior and the non-believers the inferior party. However, in his seventh proposition, Grotius makes an exception to this rule: 'It is permissible for the faithful to lend his services to the faithless'.[335] Grotius refers to the *locatio-conductio* contract of Roman law, which was, among other things, a labor-contract or a contract for lending services.[336] If the believers conclude such contracts with non-believers, they have a duty not to endanger the Christian faith, in accordance with Grotius's second premise. This implies that they should refrain from entering into contracts that entail the risk of apostasy (however, contrary to what Borschberg states, it does not mean that they may one-sidedly 'break' or terminate existing contracts).[337] To prove his proposition, Grotius refers to the examples of Joseph, who served as an overseer of the house of Pharaoh, and Daniel, who lent his services to the infidel king Nebuchadnezzar.[338] Grotius also mentions a passage from Paul's Letter to the

333 Grotius, *De societate*, fol. 317^{v}, concl. 7.

334 Grotius, *Remonstrantie*, fol. 5^{v}, pp. 76–77, trans., p. 202.

335 Grotius, *De societate*, fol. 317^{v}, prop. 7.

336 *Dig.* 19.2; cf. Borschberg, 'De societate', p. 382.

337 Borschberg, 'De societate', p. 383.

338 Gen. 39.4 and Dan. 1.4. Other examples that are mentioned are Ezra, Nehemiah and Joseph. See the references in ibid., fol. 317^{v}, sub prop. 7. The examples of Joseph and Daniel are also discussed in Vitoria, *De potestate civili*, 1, 5, § 8.

Philippians, which suggests that the household of the (pagan) Roman emperors had included Christian saints.[339] The examples mentioned by Grotius all pertain to believers of particularly strong convictions, such as Christian saints, who are not at risk of losing their faith because of their dependence on infidel employers (even if they are kings or emperors). However, the proposition that the believers may lend their services to non-believers does not necessarily apply to ordinary believers, who may be of 'weak conviction', and thus exposed to the risk of apostasy. As Grotius implies, the believers should refuse to work for infidel employers if they are at risk of losing their faith.

By contrast, those subjected to slavery do not have the possibility of refusing to work for non-Christian masters.[340] Indeed, as Grotius emphasizes in his eighth proposition, '[i]f a faithful [slave] is a slave [*servus*] of an unfaithful master, he must remain so'.[341] To prove that Christian slaves have a duty to stay with their non-Christian masters Grotius refers to a passage from Paul's first letter to Timothy, where the Apostle admonishes servants 'under the yoke' to honor their masters.[342] According to Grotius, Christian servants and slaves are thus in general required to obey their non-Christian masters. However, Grotius also maintains that the magistrate may issue a law prohibiting non-Christians from having Christians as their slaves. In this context, he refers to a statute from the Codex Theodosianus, according to which 'no heretic, infidel or Jew may keep, possess, or circumcise a Christian as a slave'.[343] In his *Remonstrantie*, Grotius mentions the same Roman statute, observing that it 'was expressly forbidden by the ancient emperors that Jews kept Christians as their slaves'.[344] He explains that when the use of slaves began to decline, the laws prohibiting Jews from having Christian slaves were analogously applied to domestic servants, in the sense that Jews were not allowed to employ Christian servants or maids

339 Philipp. 4.22: 'All the saints salute you, chiefly they that are of Caesar's household'.

340 Borschberg, 'De societate', p. 383.

341 Grotius, *De societate*, fol. 317v, prop. 8: 'Fidelis si sit servus Infidelis domini talis manere debet'.

342 1Tim. 6.1: 'Let as many servants as are under the yoke count their own masters worthy of all honour, that the name of God and his doctrine be not blasphemed'.

343 *C. ne Christ. manc. L. unica.* This law can be found in *Cod.* 1.10.1, which was originally compiled from *Cod. Th.* 16.9.1.2 and 4. The title 'ne Christ[ianum] manc[ipium]' in *Cod.* 1.10.1 consists of two laws, a rescript of emperor Constantius and a decree of emperor Justinian. The reference to 'L[ex] unica' shows that Grotius must have used the vulgate version of the Codex, which did not include Justinian's decree. See, e.g., *Codicis DN. Iustiniani* (Lugduni: Apud Hugonem a Porta, 1572), 130. The reference can be found in Grotius, *De societate*, fol. 317v, sub prop. 8.

344 Grotius, *Remonstrantie*, fol. 27 [=28], pp. 166–167, trans., p. 213 (sub art. 29–31), where he refers to the relevant laws in the *Cod.* and *Cod. Th.*

in their households.[345] In a note, Grotius distinguishes between those situations in which Christians lend their services inside the homes of their Jewish employers, and those in which they are allowed to work outside their employers' homes. If they are working inside the homes of their Jewish employers, there is a greater risk that they will be induced to apostasy. For this reason, Jews may employ Christian midwives and wet nurses for their children, but only outside their homes.[346]

Once again, Grotius's main source seems to be Aquinas, who in his *Summa theologiae* had addressed the question whether non-believers could possess Christian servants or slaves in the context of a discussion of the more general question whether they could exercise authority and dominion (that is, rights of ownership) over the believers.[347] As Aquinas explained, unlike those hired for their services (e.g., wage laborers), 'slaves are subject to their masters for their whole lifetime, and are subject to their overseers in everything'.[348] Therefore, it is more dangerous if non-Christians possess Christian slaves than if they employ Christian wage laborers. Because of their complete dependence on their masters, slaves can more easily be forced or induced to give up their Christian faith. As Aquinas emphasized, if non-Christians *already* possessed Christian slaves, then their rights of ownership had to be respected, as divine law did not cancel the man-made laws of ownership that followed from natural reason.[349] However, to prevent apostasy, the church could issue a law invalidating existing rights of ownership of non-Christian masters over their Christian slaves.[350] In other words: Christian slaves had to stay with their non-Christian masters, unless the magistrate (or the church exercising temporal jurisdiction) issued a law invalidating non-Christian ownership of Christian slaves. In *De societate*, Grotius refers to the same biblical source as Aquinas to conclude that in general Christian slaves have a duty to stay with their non-Christian masters, unless a law has been issued prohibiting non-believers from having Christian slaves.[351]

---

345 Ibid., fol. 17^{v}, pp. 124–125, trans., p. 207, art. 29–31.

346 Ibid., fol. 27 [=28]^{v}, pp. 168–169, trans., p. 213, sub art. 29–31.

347 *S. Th.* 2 2a, q. 10, a. 10. Cf. Borschberg, 'De societate', p. 383.

348 *S. Th.* 2 2a, q. 10, a. 10, resp. ad 3.

349 *S. Th.* 2 2a, q. 10, a. 10, resp. 2.

350 As Aquinas pointed out, the papacy had issued a law (applying in the territories where it had temporal jurisdiction) that if a slave of a Jew became a Christian, he should forthwith receive his freedom, without paying a price (or, if he had been bought for sale, be offered for sale to a Christian owner within three months). *S. Th.* 2 2a, q. 10, a. 10, resp.

351 Cf. the references to 1 Tim. 6.1 in *S. Th.* 2 2a, q. 10, a. 10, ad 1 and Grotius, *De societate*, fol. 317^{r}, prop. 8.

However, according to Grotius's ninth proposition, Christians are not allowed to submit themselves voluntarily as slaves to Christian masters, and even less so to non-Christian masters, except in cases of necessity.[352] Grotius does not mention a source for his proposal. Vitoria, to which he refers elsewhere in *De societate*, had maintained that it was not lawful for Christians to enslave their fellow-Christians.[353] Vitoria had referred to slavery under the law of peoples (*ius gentium*), whereby those captured in a formal public war (as well as their children) were enslaved by their captors.[354] However, Grotius's ninth proposition in *De societate* seems to relate to a different type of slavery. As Grotius would later explain in *De iure belli ac pacis*, under natural law, one could become a slave by 'voluntarily' submitting oneself to a master, for instance, by offering oneself as a slave to one's creditors to obtain remission of one's debts.[355] In Grotius's opinion, this condition was not unduly severe, if one received nourishment and other necessities of life in return for one's (lifelong) service. Parents could even sell their children into slavery, but only in case of 'necessity'.[356] However, as Grotius suggests in the ninth proposition of *De societate*, Christians are not allowed to submit themselves in this manner as slaves to other Christians, let alone to non-believers. An exception should be made in cases of necessity, if they have no other way to preserve their lives (for instance, if they or their children would otherwise die from starvation). Crucially, Grotius implies that in such cases of urgent necessity, the believers may offer themselves as slaves to non-Christian masters. The reason is briefly explained in the reading notes: 'it is better to serve than to perish'.[357]

Like Aquinas and Vitoria, Grotius understands the question whether non-Christians may have Christian slaves as a sub-question of the more general question whether they may exercise dominion and authority over Christians. Thus, in the final conclusions of *De societate*, he draws a parallel between the

352 Grotius, *De societate*, fol. 317^{v}, prop. 9.

353 Vitoria, *De iure belli*, q. 3, a. 3, § 42.

354 In *De iure belli ac pacis*, Grotius refers to these passages in Vitoria, observing that Christians have as a whole agreed not to subject other Christians to slavery if they are captured in a just war among themselves. See *IBP*, III.7.9.

355 On slavery under natural law, see *IBP*, II.5.27–30 and III.7.1. According to Grotius, this type of slavery did not itself originate from nature (by nature nobody was a slave), but it was in accordance with natural law if it was based on a voluntary agreement. See, e.g., Gustaaf van Nifterik, 'Hugo Grotius on Slavery', *Grotiana*, 22 (2001), 233–243 (p. 236) and Gustaaf van Nifterik, 'Arguments Related to Slavery in Seventeenth-Century Dutch Legal Theory', *Tijdschrift voor Rechtsgeschiedenis*, 89 (1–2) (2021), 158–191 (pp. 168–170).

356 *IBP*, II.5.29.2.

357 Grotius, *De societate*, fol. 316 (2)^{v}, left column: 'melius servire quam interire'.

enslavement of Christians and their subjection to infidel rulers. According to his eighth conclusion, 'it is incumbent upon a faithful people to obey an infidel prince or magistrate. However, a law can be made in the state so that a prince who has become unfaithful may be deposed from his leadership'.[358] Grotius does not indicate the source of his conclusion, but it may have been Vitoria, who, in his lecture on civil power (*De potestate civili*), observed that '[i]f a Christian [ruler] apostatizes, the laws state that he forfeits all public power on the grounds of his apostasy'.[359] Moreover, just as Christians may not voluntarily submit themselves as slaves to non-Christian masters, according to Grotius's ninth conclusion, they may not voluntarily submit to infidel rulers either.[360] In a marginal note, Grotius refers to Paul's First Letter to the Corinthians: 'Dare any of you, having a matter against another, go to be judged before the unjust, and not before the saints?'[361] The same verse had been quoted by Aquinas to argue that non-believers could not exercise authority or dominion over the faithful (at least, not if it was established for the first time).[362] In addition, Grotius cites a passage from Deuteronomy, where the believers are warned not to accept a foreigner as their king, but a brother[363]—a passage also cited by Vitoria.[364] On Grotius's reading, these biblical verses demonstrate that the believers are not allowed to *voluntarily* submit themselves to an infidel prince or government, just as they are not permitted to *voluntarily* submit themselves as slaves to a non-Christian master.

Grotius's ninth conclusion that the believers may not voluntarily submit to an infidel ruler is followed by an amplification and three limitations. The amplification is based on the distinction made in his seventh premise: Christians may not voluntarily submit to the authority of non-Christian rulers, and even less so to that of heretics and apostates.[365] Apart from the risk that they can be forced or induced by an infidel ruler to give up their faith, there is a 'special reason' not to submit to apostates and heretics, for they must be encouraged to repent.[366] Grotius also proposes three limitations to his conclusion. The first is that it does not seem to be forbidden that the believers entrust themselves to the

358 Ibid., fol. 317^{v}, concl. 8.

359 Vitoria, *De potestate civili*, 1, 6, § 9 (trans. in Vitoria, *Political Writings*, ed. by Anthony Pagden and Jeremy Lawrance, p. 17).

360 Grotius, *De societate*, fol. 317^{v}, concl. 9.

361 1 Cor. 6.1. Cf. ibid., fol. 317^{v}, sub concl. 9.

362 *S. Th.* 2 2ae, q. 10, a. 10.

363 Deut. 17.15. Cf. Grotius, *De societate*, fol. 317^{v}, sub concl. 9.

364 Vitoria, *De potestate civili*, 1, 5, § 8.

365 Grotius, *De societate*, fol. 317^{v}, ampl. to concl. 9.

366 Cf. ibid., fol. 315^{v}, prop. 3, lim. 1.

protection of infidel rulers if they can thereby 'save [their] religion and some freedom'.[367] Grotius gives the examples of Jacob, who had entrusted himself and his people to Pharaoh,[368] and Solomon, who had made some of his people tributary to king Hiram in exchange for the delivery of cedar trees, which were needed to build a temple for God.[369] A second limitation follows from Grotius's fifth premise: the believers may be required by a 'special command of God' to submit to the authority of infidel rulers.[370] Grotius gives the example of the Jews, who were ordered by God to serve the king of Assyria.[371] The third limitation is formulated more cautiously: the believers may 'probably' submit to infidel rulers in 'case of necessity', if doing so is the only way to preserve their lives.[372] The parallels with Grotius's treatment of slavery are clear: just as the believers are not allowed to submit themselves as slaves to non-Christian masters, unless they are forced to do so by an urgent necessity, they may not submit to the authority of an infidel prince or magistrate either, except in case of necessity, if they would otherwise be killed. With these reflections on slavery and the state, Grotius ends his treatise on public societies with non-believers.

8 Conclusion: Grotius's Contribution

Although Grotius was not the first to devote attention to the question if and to what degree it was permissible for Christians to enter into legal partnerships with non-Christians, he was the first to address this question in a comprehensive and systematic manner. By bringing together insights from older legal and theological debates on such diverse topics as marriage, slavery, almsgiving, usury, and just war, he attempted to articulate the underlying principles that governed public and private partnerships between Christians and non-Christians. As Grotius emphasized in *De societate*, 'errors of faith' did not diminish the rights and obligations that existed under the law of nature: this implied that Christians could have legal obligations and rights towards non-Christians and even heretics. Grotius concluded that, under natural and divine law, it was permissible for the believers to enter into private and public partnerships with non-believers as long as it did not undermine the authority of God or the Christian religion. These partnerships were based, not only on the natural

367 Ibid., fol. 317^{v}, concl. 9, lim 1.
368 Gen. 46.1–34 and 47.1–12.
369 1 Reg. 5.1–12, according to the verse numbering in the Vulgate, and 9.12.
370 Grotius, *De societate*, fol. 317^{v}, concl. 9, lim. 2.
371 Jer. 27.8.
372 Grotius, *De societate*, fol. 317^{v}, concl. 9, lim. 3.

duty to protect others from harm, but also on the religious obligation to treat all human beings, including those of other creeds, as neighbours. However, according to Grotius, partnerships with non-believers were not permissible if they entailed the risk of apostasy: for that reason, Christians were not allowed to voluntarily submit themselves as slaves or subjects to the authority of non-Christian masters or rulers. Moreover, preference had to be given to the faithful over non-believers, and ties of friendship and familiarity with heretics had to be avoided. Under these conditions, public and private partnerships with non-believers and heretics were permissible and even commendable.

Grotius's main contribution in *De societate* was to provide a new justification for *military* alliances between Christians and non-Christians. Medieval jurists and theologians had focused on the question whether it was permissible for Christians to use the aid of non-Christians in a war against other Christians.[373] As we have seen, they had generally condemned such alliances, especially if they were aimed against Christians. However, an exception was made in cases of 'urgent necessity', when the aid of non-Christians was necessary to defend one's own life and possessions. The sixteenth-century Spanish scholastics had proved less reluctant to accept military alliances with non-Christians, as they recognized their importance for empire-building in Asia and the Americas. According to Vitoria, the believers were generally allowed to enter into military alliances with non-believers, not only to protect their own rights, but also to protect the rights of their (infidel) allies. However, Vitoria had referred to alliances with non-Christians that were aimed against other non-Christians, and he had not discussed alliances aimed against Christians. By contrast, in *De societate*, Grotius concluded that an alliance for protecting the 'infidels' from oppression could also be justified if it was aimed against Christians, or, as he carefully put it, against those who 'wish to be considered as faithful.'[374] As Grotius explained, the duty to protect non-Christians from oppression originated from natural law, which applied irrespective of religious 'errors'. It was confirmed by the Gospel, as Christ himself had taught the believers to extend their good deeds to all human beings, including the most alien.[375] Hence, Christians had a duty to protect non-Christians from unjust oppression, even if those who oppressed them were Christians.

Grotius's justification of military alliances with non-Christians was no doubt prompted by his attempts to defend the Dutch policies of treaty and alliance-making in Asia and the East Indies.[376] As Grotius had explained in *De iure*

373 Tuck, 'Alliances with Infidels', p. 63.

374 Grotius, *De societate*, fol. 317ʳ, concl. 3.

375 Ibid., fol. 315ʳ, prop. 2, ampl.

376 Borschberg, 'De societate', pp. 389 and 392; Tuck, 'Alliances with Infidels', pp. 75–76.

praedae, Christians (e.g., the VOC) had the right to enter into military alliances with non-Christians (e.g., the king of Johor), even if they were directed against other Christians (e.g., the Spaniards and the Portuguese).[377] In Grotius's understanding, the VOC's alliances with East-Indian rulers were essentially *defensive* alliances, which served to defend the rights of the Dutch (e.g., the rights to free navigation and trade) as well as those of their non-Christian allies (e.g., the right not to be unjustly oppressed). Grotius referred to the VOC's alliances with East-Indian rulers in a memorandum which he prepared in 1607 in view of the peace negotiations between the Dutch Republic and Spain. As he pointed out, the VOC had entered into these alliances on behalf of the Dutch Estates General; if a peace agreement with Spain would force the VOC to end its activities in the East Indies, then its allies would be left unprotected, which would seriously harm the Dutch reputation.[378] In the context of the peace negotiations, Grotius's defense of military alliances with non-Christians could thus serve to convince the Estates General (as well as international audiences) to support the outcome desired by the VOC directors, namely that the conclusion of a peace treaty with Spain should not force them to give up the East-Indian trade.

However, in *De societate*, Grotius not only contributed to the debate about treaties and alliances with non-Christian rulers in the East-Indian context. He also intervened in the domestic debate about the legal conditions under which non-Christian minorities (e.g., Jews) could be admitted to the Dutch Republic. As Grotius emphasized in *De societate*, the 'highest public partnership' was the 'union of the state', and there was 'no doubt' that Christians could live together in one state with non-Christians.[379] Building on Cicero's definition of the state as an 'association' that originated from nature itself, Grotius argued that it could encompass both the faithful and non-believers. He concluded that it was generally permissible for a Christian government to 'accept an infidel people under its authority'.[380] Indeed, if non-Christians were admitted to a Christian state, it was more likely that they would convert to Christianity than if they remained subject to non-Christian rulers. In his *Remonstrantie*, Grotius would use these same arguments to advocate the admission of Jews to the Dutch provinces. The principal reason for admitting the Jews was that it would contribute to their *voluntary* conversion to Christianity, which would not come about if the Jews were 'cut off from the conversation with Christians'.[381] As Grotius concluded,

377 *IPC*, ed. Hamaker, p. 298, ed. Van Ittersum, p. 434.
378 Grotius, *Vertoog*, fol. 406^r.
379 Grotius, *De societate*, fol. 317^r, concl. 5.
380 Ibid., fol. 317^v, concl. 7.
381 Grotius, *Remonstrantie*, fol. 5^v, pp. 76–77, trans., p. 202 (trans. modified).

under natural and divine law, the states of Holland had a duty to offer protection to the Jews, irrespective of their 'errors of faith'. The arguments that applied to alliances between the believers and non-believers in the East-Indian context thus also applied in the domestic context: Christians had a duty to protect non-Christians from unjust oppression, even if those who oppressed them were Christians.

Grotius also used some of the arguments he had developed in *De societate* in *De iure belli ac pacis*. In chapter 15 of book 2, he returned to the 'frequently discussed question' whether Christians were allowed to enter into treaties with 'those who are strangers to the true religion'. As Grotius explained, it was 'in no degree a matter of doubt' that such treaties were permissible under the law of nature, because 'the right to enter into treaties is so common to all men that it does not admit of a distinction arising from religion'.[382] However, it was more questionable whether treaties with non-believers were allowed under Christian law. Recalling one of the main conclusions of *De societate*, Grotius observed that it was generally permissible under Hebraic law to make treaties with non-believers to prevent harm, mentioning the treaty between Jacob and Laban as example.[383] Treaties of friendship and trade were permissible as well, as was proven by David and Solomon's treaties with Hiram.[384] Grotius continued by quoting Juvenal's critique of the Jews, who had refused to show strangers the way to a well, explaining that 'the example of pointing out the way stands for the benefits [*beneficia*] which are least troublesome and costly, which Cicero and Seneca say ought to be granted even to strangers'.[385] Exactly the same combination of sources—Juvenal, Cicero and Seneca—had been discussed in *De societate* to support the proposition that the believers should do good, i.e., provide assistance and protection, to non-believers.[386] As Grotius argued in *De iure belli ac pacis*, 'alliances for purposes of war' were permissible as well, as was demonstrated by the example of Abraham who had provided military assistance to the 'impious Sodomites'.[387] It was true that the Old Testament also mentioned examples of rulers who had been punished for allying with non-believers, but, on Grotius's reading, these were exceptions to the general rule that alliances with non-believers were allowed by divine and natural law.[388]

382 *IBP*, II.15.8.
383 *IBP*, II.15.9.1.
384 *IBP*, II.15.9.2.
385 *IBP*, II.15.9.3 (trans. modified).
386 *IBP*, II.15.9.3. Cf. Grotius, *De societate*, fol. 314^v–315^r, prop. 2, ampl.
387 *IBP*, II.15.9.6.
388 For instance, the alliance of Asa with the Syrians was condemned because of a fault in the intentions with which it was made (Asa had distrusted God). See *IBP*, II.15.9.9.

There are also clear parallels between *De societate* and the section in *De iure belli ac pacis*, in which Grotius examined whether treaties with 'those who are strangers to the true religion' were in accordance with the Gospel. He began by observing that the law of the Gospel had not changed Hebraic law, in the sense that it remained permissible for the believers to make alliances with non-believers. Citing the Sermon on the Mount, and referring to Vitoria (amongst others),[389] Grotius explained that the law of the Gospel had extended 'even greater favor to treaties by which those who are strangers to the true religion receive help in a just cause; for the doing of good to all men, whenever there is opportunity, has not only been left free and praiseworthy, but has even been enjoined by precept'.[390] His phrase echoed one of the main conclusions of *De societate*: doing good to all men, including those of other creeds, was not merely a right, but depending on the circumstances, it could also be an obligation. However, the obligation to do good to non-believers was not without limitations: thus, preference had to be given to the faithful over non-believers: 'we should be doers of good to all, but particularly to those who share the same religion'.[391] Moreover, cultivating ties of friendship and familiarity with heretics and apostates was allowed only if it 'furnishe[d] the hope of their correction'.[392] Exactly the same limitations had been formulated in *De societate*.[393] In *De iure belli ac pacis*, Grotius made the permissibility of partnerships with non-believers subject to the same conditions he had proposed in *De societate:* the believers were not allowed to *voluntarily* submit themselves to the authority of non-believers or to conclude marriages with them, as it might lead to apostasy.[394] For that same reason, 'too great intimacy' (e.g., living together) with non-believers had to be avoided, so that it did not bring 'contamination to the weak'.[395] Grotius recalled the premise he had formulated in *De societate*: it was never permissible to engage in partnerships with non-believers that could harm the authority of God and the Christian religion: '[f]or as a matter of first importance the kingdom of heaven is to be sought, that is, the spread of the Gospel'.[396]

---

389 The reference is to Vitoria, *De Indis*, q. 3, a. 5, §15 and a. 7, §17. Other authors to which Grotius refers in this context are Franciscus Arias, Cajetanus and Luis de Molina. Cf. *IBP*, II.15.9.1.

390 *IBP*, II.15.10.

391 *IBP*, II.15.10.2.

392 *IBP*, II.15.10.3.

393 Grotius, *De societate*, fol. 315^{v}, prop. 3, lim. 2 and 3.

394 *IBP*, II.15.10.4.

395 *IBP*, II.15.11.1.

396 Math. 6.33, quoted in *IBP*, II.15.11.2. Cf. Grotius, *De societate*, fol. 314^{r}, prem. 2.

However, notwithstanding these parallels, there was also an important difference between the conclusions presented in *De societate* and *De iure belli ac pacis*. As we have seen, one of the main conclusions in *De societate* had been that Christians were allowed to enter into military alliances with non-Christians, even if they were aimed against other Christians. The faithful could thus wage a just war to protect non-believers from unjust oppression, even if those who oppressed them were themselves Christians.[397] Strikingly, this conclusion from *De societate* did not reappear in *De iure belli ac pacis*. Instead, Grotius quoted Fulk, the Archbishop of Reims (883–900), who had warned Charles the Simple not to enter into alliances with the 'enemies of God', arguing that it made 'no difference whether any one allies himself with the heathen or denies God and worships idols'.[398] The implication was that Christians were *not* allowed to use the assistance of non-Christians in a war against their fellow-believers.[399] Moreover, Grotius now maintained that all Christians had a duty to contribute to a league against the enemies of Christianity.[400] While one of Grotius's main conclusions in *De societate* had been that Christians could enter into military alliances with non-Christians, even against other Christians, in *De iure belli ac pacis*, he emphasized the duty of the faithful to join a league with their fellow-believers against the 'infidels'. He gave the example of the league that had been made 'under the leadership of the emperor of the Holy Roman Empire', perhaps a reference to the league formed by Frederick III of Habsburg and the papacy against the Turks, after the fall of Constantinople.[401] Although Grotius still defended military alliances with non-Christians in non-European contexts (e.g., the VOC's alliances with native rulers in Asia and the East Indies),[402] he now explicitly rejected such alliances in the European context, calling instead for a league of all Christian nations against the 'enemies of Christianity' (e.g., the Ottoman empire).[403]

---

397 Grotius, *De societate*, fol. 317^r, concl. 3.

398 *IBP*, II.15.11.3.

399 In the next sentence, Grotius quoted Alexander the Great saying that '[t]hey do a grievous wrong against the rights of Greeks who serve with the barbarians in war against Greeks'. *IBP*, II.15.11.3.

400 *IBP*, II.15.12.

401 This is suggested by Johannes Gronovius in Grotius, *De iure belli ac pacis libri tres* (Amsterdam: Ex officina Wetsteniana, 1720), p. 434 (n. 71); Condorelli, 'Grotius's Doctrine of Alliances', p. 31.

402 Van Ittersum, 'The Long Goodbye', pp. 391–393; Van Hulle, 'Grotius, Informal Empire', pp. 48–52.

403 This shift of emphasis—from a justification of military alliances with non-Christians in *De societate* to a defense of a league against the enemies of Christianity in *De iure belli*

The similarities and differences between Grotius's *De societate* and his other writings (including *De iure belli ac pacis*) allow us to trace the development of his ideas about alliances with non-Christians. As we have seen, in *De iure praedae*, Grotius's aim had been to defend the VOC's policies of alliance-making in the East Indies, and more specifically, the seizure of a Portuguese vessel, the Santa Catarina, as a just prize taken on behalf of a non-Christian ally, the Sultan of Johor. As Grotius explained, the right to enter into alliances with non-Christians followed from the natural laws of non-offensiveness and protection, which prescribed that others should be protected from harm, irrespective of religious differences. In the context of the peace negotiations with Spain, Grotius drafted a second treatise, *De societate publica cum infidelibus*, in which he explained why public partnerships with non-Christians—including military alliances—were allowed not only by natural law, but also by Christian law: the natural duty to protect others from harm was confirmed by the Gospel, according to which all human beings should be treated as neighbours and children of God. As we have seen, Grotius's aim was no longer only to justify the VOC's policies of alliance-making in the East Indies, but to write a more general treatise on private and public partnerships with non-Christians, which was also relevant to the domestic debate about religious minorities in the Dutch Republic. Thus, in his *Remonstrantie*, he referred to the natural duty to protect non-Christians from oppression to argue that the States of Holland and West-Friesland had an obligation to offer a refuge to the Jews. Finally, in *De iure belli ac pacis*, Grotius focused on the European context, arguing that all Christians (i.e., Catholic *and* Protestant nations) had a duty to join a league against the enemies of Christianity. As an exile in Paris, his hope was that if all Christian nations would join a league against the Ottomans, it would contribute to overcoming the internal divisions of Christianity, thus laying the foundations for a lasting peace in Europe.[404]

---

ac pacis—can perhaps be explained from the context. By the time Grotius wrote *De iure belli ac pacis*, he was living in Paris, supported by a pension from Louis XIII. As an exile in Paris, he had to take into account French sensitivities regarding the VOC's activities in the East Indies (Louis XIII had his own plans for founding a French East India Company, which would compete with the Dutch VOC) as well as domestic tensions relating to the Huguenots. Hence, instead of openly defending the VOC's alliances with non-Christian rulers or the rights of religious minorities, he now emphasized the obligation of all Christians to contribute to a league against the Turks.

404 Cf. Condorelli, 'Grotius's Doctrine of Alliances', p. 31.

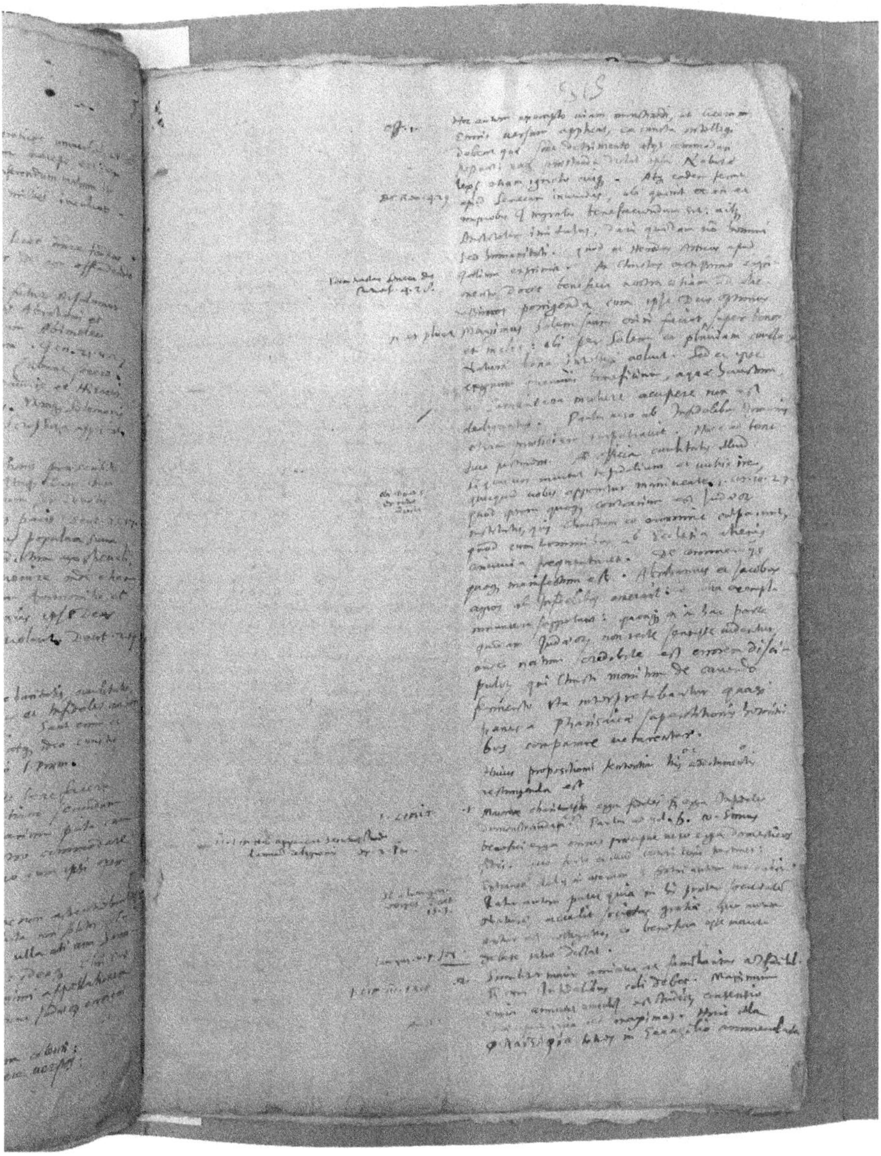

FIGURE 2 Third page of *De societate publica cum infidelibus*, written in the hand of Grotius. This page contains an explanation of the second proposition, followed by three limitations, which have been renumbered by Grotius. The old numbering is still visible. Leiden University Library, MS BPL 922 Ie, fol. 315r.

Synopsis

314r **Introd.** Main question: if and to what degree it should be allowed to Christians to enter into a partnership with non-believers, or even heretics

Prem. 1 An 'error of faith' does not change those things that pertain to natural law

Prem. 2 One must avoid all things that appear to go against divine glory and the true religion

Prem. 3 Even in things that are generally permitted, we should distinguish what is decent from what is offending

Prem. 4 If extreme urgency compels us, many things are done justly that are otherwise unjust

Prem. 5 Things that are generally called just or unjust sometimes cease to be so due to a special calling

Prem. 6 Many actions that are not unlawful in themselves are condemned because of the inner state of mind of the actor

Prem. 7 Distinction between those who belong to the Church and those who do not

Prem. 8 Distinctions between different types of alliance: *ἐπιμαχία/ συμμαχία*, private/ public, equal/unequal, superior/ inferior

Prem. 9 An alliance for purposes of war can be just

Prem. 10 Universal [alliance] should not be just without exception

314v **Prop. 1** To refrain from harming non-believers and heretics in general is not only permissible, but even necessary (from prem. 1)

Concl. 1 It is permissible for both private and public persons to enter into a pact with non-believers or heretics with the aim not to harm one another

Prop. 2 Good deeds, duties, and trades may rightly be cultivated between the believers and non-believers or heretics, as they also originate from nature (as in prem. 1)

Ampl. It is not only allowed to do good to non-believers or heretics, but according to the circumstances even necessary, when we can help them without great disadvantage, or when they ask our help themselves

315r The idea of this proposition should be restricted by these additions:
1 lim. [1]: Greater charity must be shown towards the faithful than towards the unfaithful

2. lim. (ex prem. 2): Unless it appears to harm the [true] faith. Usury may be taken from a stranger, but not from a brother. The closer the connection, the greater the benefits should be
1 lim. prop. 3 [2]:[1] Likewise greater friendship and familiarity should be cultivated with the faithful than with the non-believers

315^{v} **1 prem. in prop.:**
In prop.: There are two kinds of non-believers or *ἑτεροδόξοι*: those who never belonged to the Church and those who have departed from it, or are expelled by an ecclesiastical judgement
2 lim. prop. 3: Christians must abstain from intimate relations and social intercourse with those who have fallen from the Church or have been condemned by its judgement. However, this does not apply in case of necessity, or even utility, when heretics are approached with the hope of conversion
3 lim. ex prem. 3: One should not enter into a very close familiarity with non-believers or heretics without reason: those who converse with non-Christians should take care on all occasions, so that they try to bring them to good sense by doctrine and example
Let us first consider equal partnerships, of which there are different degrees

Prop. 3 It is permissible to have some friendship and familiarity with non-believers and heretics

Prop. 4 The highest union is in marriage. In case of a concluded marriage, it is not permissible to separate from a non-believer
Lim.: However, it is permissible for a faithful magistrate to make a law by which the marriage of a faithful person with an unbeliever is invalidated, but only for just reasons

Prop. 5 Marriages with non-believers that are still to be concluded should be condemned, because the main purpose of marriage is the education of children to the glory of God, which is not a little hindered by such marriages
Lim.: An exception should be made in case of a special calling (which may perhaps be said of Esther)

317^{r} Public alliances

Concl. 2 Treaties with non-believers are rightly entered into for the sake of friendship, commerce, travels, and other benefits which are mutually guaranteed

1 Here, Grotius changed the numbering. The original numbering is placed between brackets.

Lim.: Unless there is a special reason, for instance, in case of apostasy

In prem.: There are two kinds of military alliances: defensive and offensive. Such alliances are unjust if war is agreed to without exception, unless the cause is just

Concl. 3 In a just war, the non-believers are rightly defended by the faithful, even if those who oppress the non-believers consider themselves as faithful. This work is not only permitted, but also highly praiseworthy, and because of the circumstances often necessary

Lim.: An exception should be made if God wants to punish particular nations for infidelity

Concl. 4 If they fight a just war, the faithful may use the help of non-believers. Conditions: 1. As long as no occasion is thereby offered to the non-believers for harming the truth; 2. As long as it is not done out of distrust or against a special command

Concl. 5 The highest public partnership is the union of the state. A faithful people can remain in one state with non-believers

Concl. 6 However, whether a [faithful] people may voluntarily enter into such a community with non-believers is more difficult to say. An analogy can be made with marriage. Thus, sharing a state with non-believers should be avoided outside cases of necessity, and especially with those who have departed from the Church

Prop. 6 It is permissible for the faithful to have non-believers as servants and even as slaves

317v **Conc. 7** It is equally permissible for a faithful magistrate or people to accept an infidel people under its authority

Prop. 7 It is permissible for a faithful [person] to lend his services to non-believers

Prop. 8 A faithful [slave] who is a slave of an unfaithful master must remain so. However, the magistrate may issue a law prohibiting non-believers from having the faithful as slaves

Prop. 9 It is not easily allowed to submit oneself voluntarily in slavery to a believer, and even less so to a non-believer. However, in case of necessity, it does not seem to be prohibited

Concl. 8 A faithful people has a duty to obey an infidel prince or magistrate. However, a law can be made in the state to depose a prince who has become unfaithful

Concl. 9 It is hardly permissible [for a believer] to submit to such [an infidel ruler]

Ampl. It is less permissible to submit to an apostate than to a non-believer
Lim.: It does not seem to be forbidden to place oneself under the protection of an infidel [ruler], in order to save religion and some freedom
Lim.: It is permissible (even without exception) to submit oneself to a non-believer where there is a special command of God
Lim.: It is (probably) permissible to submit to a non-believer in case of urgent necessity

Editorial Principles

1. Exact transliteration of the text of Grotius's treatise, with a few exceptions:
   - u/v: according to modern usage; consonantal u is printed as v, v used as a vowel is printed as u
   - i/j: the letter j has been changed in i in all Latin words.
2. All accents in the Latin text have been omitted.
3. Punctuation has been adapted to modern usage.[1]
4. Grotius's capitals have been retained, except for sentences after a period, which always open with a capital.
5. Words or letters between square brackets [ ] are additions by the editors.
6. Round brackets ( ) are printed as found in the text or are silently added in a few cases for the sake of clarity.
7. Textual commentary has been added to the Latin transcription, historical commentary to the English translation.

1 'In matters of punctuation one should unhesitatingly adopt modern principles ...'. See the section 'Spelling and Punctuation', in Jozef IJsewijn and Dirk Sacré, *Companion to Neo-Latin Studies, Part II: Literary, Linguistic, Philological and Editorial Questions* (Leuven: Leuven University Press, 1998), pp. 472–475.

 | DOI:10.1163/9789004744592_004

Transcription and Translation

De societate publica cum infidelibus (Leiden, University Library, MS Cod. BPL 922)

XVIII N 922 Ie
Fol. 314–318: Hugonis Grotii Theses autographae de Societate cum infidelibus publica; accedunt Adversaria huc pertinentia, folia 6.[1]

314r De societate publica[2] cum infidelibus

Vetus est quaestio et nostra hac aetate non minus agitata, an et quatenus hominibus Christianis liceat cum Infidelibus, aut etiam Haereticis inire societatem. Ea videtur a plerisque exemplis magis quam rationibus, ac praeterea non satis distincte esse tractata. Quare tentandum arbitramur an ei lux aliqua nova discussione afferri possit. Antequam autem ad argumentum veniamus haec praefabimur.

1. Cum duplex sit Humani generis societas, altera ex creatione, altera ex recreatione, sive naturalis et Ecclesiastica, et ad prioris illius conservationem institutum sit Ius illud quod Naturae dicimus, tum primarium, tum secundarium, sciendum est errorem in fide nihil eorum immutare quae ad ius Naturae et universalis illius societatis tuitionem pertinent, quo argumento utitur Thomas 2[a], 2[ae], quaest[io] 10, art[iculus] 10.[3]

2. Omnia ea quae apparet adversatura divinae gloriae et verae religioni adeo distincte sunt[4] cavenda, ut neque spes, neque metus ullus contra persuadeat. Sed maneat illud: Quaerite primum regnum caelorum.

3. Etiam in his quae in universum libertati nostrae permittuntur maxima est habenda ratio[5] eius quod deceat, aut offendat.

1 Title, added on the flyleaf by a later hand.
2 'publica' added above the line. The title is in capitals.
3 After the reference to Thomas Grotius deleted two words: 'Quare eam'.
4 'sunt' above the line.
5 First Grotius wrote: 'maximam esse habendam rationem'.

 | DOI:10.1163/9789004744592_005

On Public Partnership with Non-Believers (Leiden, University Library, MS Cod. BPL 922)

XVIII N 922 IE

Fol. 314–318: Autograph theses of Hugo Grotius On public partnership with non-believers; with added notes pertaining to the matter, 6 folio sheets.

314r On public partnership with non-believers.

It is an old question, and also in our days frequently discussed, if and to what degree it be allowed to Christians to enter into a partnership with non-believers, or even heretics. The question appears to be treated on the basis of multiple examples, rather than reasons, and moreover not with sufficient distinctions. Therefore we think it necessary to try whether some light may be shed on it by a new discussion. Before we come to the argument, let us declare these things in advance.

1. Since the community of mankind is of two types, one stemming from creation, the other from recreation, that is, the natural and the ecclesiastical, and for the preservation of the former one a law is instituted that we call [the law] of nature (either primary or secondary), it should be known that an error of faith changes nothing of those things that pertain to natural law and the protection of that universal community, an argument used by Thomas 2[a], 2[ae], quaest[io] 10, art[iculus] 10.[1]

2. One must therefore carefully guard against all things that appear to go against divine glory and the true religion, so that neither hope, nor fear will advise the contrary. Let this admonition however remain: first of all, seek the kingdom of heaven.[2]

3. Also in those affairs that are permitted to our liberty in general, one should first and foremost take into account what is decent or offending.

1 See the reference to *S. Th.* 2a 2ae, q. 10, a. 10 in the reading notes on fol. 316 (2)v, left column, and in *IBP*, II.15.8 (ed. Feenstra, p. 395, n. 3).

2 Math. 6.33. Cf. *IBP*, II.15.11.2 (ed. Feenstra, p. 401), with the reference to Math. 6.33 in n. 8: 'Quaerendum enim primo loco est regnum celeste, id est Evangelii propagatio.'

4. Sed tamen in his ipsis si extrema necessitas urgeat multa recte fiunt[1] quae alioqui vitio non carerent.

5. Tenenda est et haec generalis exceptio quae iusta aut iniusta dicuntur, talia interdum esse desinere ob specialem vocationem.

6. Ac multas actiones per se non illicitas damnari propter internam constitutionem animi facientis. 2 Sam. 33; 2 Reg. 20 in fine.

7. Dist[inctio] Inf[idelium] 1:[2] alii ad Ecclesiam pertinuerunt,[3] alii non.

8. De societate duplici: ἐπιμ[αχία], συμ[μαχία]. Societas Privata—publica; aequalis—inaequalis; Superior—Inferior.

9. Societas bellica iusta esse potest.

10. Universalis sine exceptione iusta esse non sit.

314^{v} His praemissis prima sit propositio:

1. Prop[ositio]. Abstinere a noxa in Infideles, et haereticos universaliter non modo licet Christianis sed etiam necesse est; ex primo Praemisso. Nemini enim inferendum malum lex Naturae praecipit, idque Christus millies inculcat. Unde sequitur Conclusio:

1. Concl[usio]. Tum privatis tum publicis personis licet inire foedus cum Infidelibus aut Haereticis de non offendendo utrinque.
Quicquid enim recte fit idem recte futurum stipulamur et promittimus. Tale fuit foedus Abrahami et postea Isaaci, piorum hominum, cum Abimeleco pro-

---

1 'fiunt': written in a scrawled hand. Possibly Grotius wrote: 'fient'.

2 The reading of '1', to be interpreted as '1a' or 'prima', is uncertain. The 'praemissa' numbers 7–10 seem to have been hastily added at a later stage.

3 'pertinuerunt': this word is hard to decipher because of Grotius's poor handwriting. Perhaps Grotius intended to write: 'ad Ecclesiam pertinentes'. See further on, fol. 315^{v} (beginning) and Grotius's reading notes, fol. 316 (2)^{v}, left column.

4. But even in these affairs, however, if extreme urgency compels us, many things are done justly that otherwise would not be devoid of error.

5. This general exception must be made, that things that are called just or unjust, sometimes cease to be thus due to a special calling.

6. And that many actions that are not illicit in themselves are condemned as the result of the inner state of mind of the one who performs them. 2 Sam. 33;[1] 2 Reg. 20 at the end.

7. Distinction between non-believers 1: some belonged to the Church, others did not.

8. On two types of alliance: ἐπιμ[αχία] [defensive], συμ[μαχία] [offensive].[2] Private alliance—public; equal—unequal; superior—inferior.

9. An alliance for purposes of war can be just.

10. A general [alliance] should not be just without exception.

314v After these premisses, let the first proposition be:

1. Proposition. To refrain from harming non-believers and heretics in general is not only permissible for Christians, but also necessary; from the first premise. For the law of nature prescribes that evil should be inflicted on no one, and Christ emphasizes this a thousand times. Hence follows the conclusion:

1. Conclusion. It is permissible for both private and public persons to enter into a pact with non-believers or heretics not to harm one another.
For whatever is rightly done, we stipulate and promise that the same will be right in the future. Such was the pact of Abraham, and afterwards of Isaac, pious

1 2 Sam. 33: this Bible book has only 24 chapters. Perhaps Grotius referred to 2 Sam. [14].33. 2 Reg. 20.19 deals with Hizkia, who paid scant attention to Isaiah's warnings. But see also *IBP*, II.15.9.9 (ed. Feenstra, p. 399, n. 4 and 5): 'Multa enim non illicita vitiat animus, ut censum in Davide, thesaurorum ostensionem in Ezechia', with references to 2 Sam. 24 (the numbering of the people in Israel and Judah) and 2 Reg. 20.13 (Hezekiah showing his treasury to the ambassadors of the king of Babylon).

2 Cf. *DIP*, ed. Hamaker, p. 65, ed. Van Ittersum, p. 100, with a reference to Thucydides; *IBP* II.15.6.3 (ed. Feenstra, p. 393), with a reference to Thucydides and Livius. See also *De societate*, fol. 317r and Grotius's reading notes, fol. 316 (2)v.

fano Rege; idque haereditarium. Gen. 21 v. 27 et 26 v. 29. Item Iacobi cum Labane socero. Gen. 31 v. 49. Tale item Davidis et Hirami, Tyrionum Regis: 2 Sam. 5.11. Itemque Solomonis et Hirami, quod manifeste Scriptura approbat. 1 Reg. [5 v. 26]; 2 Sam. 5 v. 12.

Excipe eos fideles, qui ex vocationis praescripto tenentur Infideles punire. Itaque Deus cum Amalecitis (Deut. 17.16) et cum sex devotis populis vetat constitui foedus pacis (Deut. 25.17),[1] quia ad illos puniendos Deus populum suum elegerat. Ideoque hoc interdictum ex speciali, non ex generali causa venire inde etiam apparet, quia contra cum[2] Ammonitis et ipsis Infidelibus foedus pacis ipse Deus a populo fideli servari voluit. Deut. 2.19.

Secunda propositio sit:

II. Prop[ositio]. Beneficia, officia, commercia charitatis, civilitatis et utilitatis ergo inter Fideles et Infideles aut haer[eticos] ultro[3] citroque recte colantur. Sunt enim et haec ex Natura prodeuntia, atque ideo cunctis hominibus communia, ut in 1 Praem[isso].

Ampl[ificatio]. Adde non tantum licitum esse benefacere Infidelibus aut haer[eticis], sed etiam secundum circumstantias saepe necessarium puta, cum sine magno incommodo nostro commodare ipsis possumus, praecipue vero cum ipsi opem nostram exposcunt.

1 Grotius did not add parentheses.
2 'cum' possibly deleted.
3 Grotius first wrote 'ultroque'.

men, with the heathen king Abimelech; and that was hereditary. Gen. 21 v. 27 and 26 v. 29. Likewise of Jacob with his father-in-law Laban. Gen. 31 v. 49.[1] Such also of David and Hiram, king of Tyre: 2 Sam. 5.11.[2] And likewise of Solomon and Hiram, which Scripture clearly approves.[3] 1 Reg. [5 v. 26]; 2 Sam. 5 v. 12.

Make an exception for those believers, who are bound by the prescription of a calling to punish non-believers. And so God forbids to conclude a peace treaty with the Amalekites (Deut. 17.16)[4] and with the six cursed peoples (Deut. 25.17),[5] because God had chosen his people to punish them. And therefore, that this prohibition comes from a special, not from a general reason, also appears from the fact that, on the contrary, God himself wished that the peace treaty with the Ammonites and precisely the non-believers was to be kept by the faithful people. Deut. 2.19.[6]

Let the second proposition be:

II. Proposition. Good deeds, duties, trades, for the sake of charity, civility, and utility,[7] can be rightly cultivated reciprocally between the faithful and the non-believers or heretics. For these things also proceed from nature, and are therefore common to all men, as in the first premise.

Amplification. Add to this that it is not only allowed to do good to non-believers or heretics, but according to the circumstances, consider it even necessary, when we can help them without great disadvantage to ourselves, especially when they ask our help themselves.

1 Grotius also discusses the treaty between Jacob and Laban in *IBP*, II.15.9.1 (ed. Feenstra, p. 395).
2 The treaty between David and Hiram is also mentioned in *IBP*, II.15.9.2 (ed. Feenstra, p. 396).
3 Cf. the reference to the treaty between Solomon and Hiram in *IBP*, II.15.9.2 (ed. Feenstra, p. 396).
4 Read: Ex. 17.16.
5 'Devotus' in the sense of 'damnatus' ('cursed') was a qualification for the five, six, seven or more peoples living in Kanaan, before the Israelites settled there. See Deut. 7.1–2; 20.17, Ex. 3.8; 3.17; 23.23, etc., and *IBP*, II.15.9.1, where Grotius refers to the 'populi septem divina sententia damnati'.
6 Cf. *IBP*, II.15.9.5 (ed. Feenstra, p. 397).
7 The three genitives seem to correspond with the three preceeding nouns, so 'beneficia charitatis, officia civilitatis, commercia utilitatis' ('good deeds of charity, duties of civility and trades of utility'). 'Charitatis' corresponds with 'beneficia' ('the good deeds of charity'), as 'charitas' is considered as the first of 'beneficia'; 'civilitatis' with 'officia' ('the duty of civility') and 'utilitas' with 'commercia' ('the utility of trade').

His positionibus Iudaei veteres non assentiebantur, quos dicit Iohannes Evangelista ([Ioh.] 4.9)[1] non solitos συγχρῆσθαι, hoc est consuetudine ulla uti cum Samaritanis, utpote ἑτεροδόξοις; ideoque Christus in Parabola ipsis ostendit proximi appellationem etiam ad hos pertinere. Luc. 10.36; Act. 10.28. Hunc Iudaeorum errorem etiam Satyra notat:

> Non monstrare vias eadem nisi sacra colenti;
> Quaesitum ad fontem solos deducere verpos.

315r Hoc autem exemplo viam monstrandi, ut Cicero[2] Ennii versum applicat (Off. 1.[51]), ea cuncta intelligi debent quae sine detrimento aliis commodari possunt; eaque praestanda dictat ipsa Naturae lex etiam ignoto cuique. Atque eadem ferme apud Senecam invenies, ubi quaerit[3] an et improbis et ingratis benefaciendum sit; aitque Aristotelem imitatus, dari quaedam non homini sed humanitati. De Ben[eficiis] 4.29. Quod et Herodes Atticus apud Gellium exprimit. Idem tractat Seneca De Benef[iciis] 4.28. Ac Christus certissimo argumento docet beneficia nostra etiam ad alienissimos porrigenda, cum ipse Deus Optimus Maximus Solem suum oriri faciat et pluat super bonos et malos: ubi per Solem et pluviam cuncta Naturae bona intelligi voluit. Sed et ipse exiguum quamvis beneficium, aquae haustum a Samaritana muliere accipere non est dedignatus. Paulus vero ab Infidelibus Romanis etiam praesidium impetravit. Haec ad beneficia pertinent. Ad officia civilitatis illud: Si quis vos invitat Infidelium, et vultis ire, quicquid vobis apponitur manducate. 1 Cor. 10.27. Obi[ectio]

1 Grotius noted '4. 9' in the margin. In the following we tacitly add parentheses when Grotius mentioned a source like a Bible verse in a running sentence.

2 After 'Cicero' Grotius deleted: 'in'.

3 After 'quaerit' Grotius deleted: 'et'.

The ancient Jews did not agree with these assertions: who, as John the Evangelist says ([Ioh.] 4.9), do not usually have dealings (συγχρῆσθαι), which means have any kind of social intercourse with the Samaritans, as the heterodox (ἑτεροδόξοι); and therefore Christ shows them in the parable that the appellation of neighbor also applies to them. Luc. 10.36; Act. 10.28.[1] Juvenal's Satire also notes this error of the Jews:

> Forbidding to point out the way to any not worshipping the same rites,
> and conducting none but the circumcised to the desired fountain.[2]

315r Now by this example of showing the way, as Cicero applies the verse of Ennius ([On] dut[ies] 1. [51]),[3] all those things must be understood which can be offered (as help) without harm to others: and the very law of nature dictates that these should be provided, even to an unknown person. And you will find almost the same things in Seneca, where he asks whether good should be done both to the wicked and the ungrateful; and following Aristotle,[4] he says that some things are not given to men, but to humanity. *On Benefits* 4.29.[5] Which also Herod Atticus expresses in [Aulus] Gellius.[6] Seneca discusses the same thing in *On Benefits* 4.28. And Christ teaches with the most certain argument that our good deeds should be extended even to the most alien people, since God himself, the Best and the Greatest, makes his sun rise for and his rain fall upon the good and the bad alike, as he wanted all the good things of nature to be understood through the sun and the rain.[7] But even he himself did not disdain to receive a drink of water from a Samaritan woman, even though it was a small benefit.[8] But Paul also obtained protection from the non-believing Romans.[9] These [examples] pertain to good deeds. For the duties of civility, this is valid: If someone of the non-believers invites you, and you want to go, eat whatever

1 These two references, placed in the left margin, fit well into Grotius's argument as they deal with Christ's refusal to distinguish between Jews and Samaritans or Gentiles.

2 Juv. *Sat.* 14.103–104. The same verse (Juv. *Sat.* 14.103) is quoted in *IBP*, II.15.9.3 (ed. Feenstra, p. 396).

3 Cic. *off.* 1.51 quotes Ennius: 'Homo, qui erranti comiter monstrat viam/ Quasi lumen de suo lumine accendat/ facit/ Nihilo minus ipsi lucet, cum illi accenderit.'

4 Cf. Diog. Laert. 5.21.

5 The references to Cic. *off.* 1.51 and Sen. *ben.* 6.9 (4.29) can also be found in *IBP*, II.15.9.3 (ed. Feenstra, p. 396, n. 5 and 6).

6 Aul. Gell. *Noct. Attic.* 9.2.7.

7 Math. 5.45. The same verse is quoted in *IBP*, II.15.10.1 (ed. Feenstra, p. 399), and Grotius, *Remonstrantie*, fol. 6v, pp. 80–81, trans., p. 202.

8 Ioh. 4.9.

9 Act. 25.25 and 26.25. Cf. *IBP*, II.15.10.4 (ed. Feenstra, p. 401).

Deut. 5 et ratio adiecta.[1] Quod ipsum quoque contrarium est Iudaeorum institutis, qui Christum eo nomine culparunt quod cum hominibus ab Ecclesia alienis convivia frequentaret. De commerciis quoque manifestum est. Abrahamus et Iacobus agros ab Infidelibus emerunt. Et alia exempla innumera suppetunt: quanquam et in hac parte quidam Iudaeorum non recte sensisse videntur, unde natum credibile est errorem discipulorum qui Christi monitum de cavendo fermento ita interpretabantur quasi panes a Pharisaicae superstitionis hominibus comparare vetarentur.

Huius propositionis sententia his additamentis[2] restringenda est.

I. Limit[atio]. 1 [*old number*].[3] Maior charitas erga fideles quam erga Infideles demonstranda est.[4] Paulus ad Gal. 6.10. Simus benefici erga omnes, praecipue vero erga domesticos fidei.

II. Lim[itatio]. Nisi appareat secuturum unde[5] damnum religionis; ex 2 P[raemissio]ne.[6] Quo forte et illud veteris legis pertinet: Extraneo dabis in usuram; fratri autem non dabis. Ab alienigena exiges, Deut. 15.3. Ratio autem patet quia in his praeter societatem Naturae, accedit societas gratiae. Quo autem arctior

---

1 'Obi[ectio] Deut. 5 et ratio adiecta': Grotius placed this reference in the margin.

2 Grotius maintained an open variant here: 'hoc additamento'.

3 Here Grotius seems to have changed the numbering. He did not cross out the original numbering in the main text, while adding the new numbering in the margins. The first limitation to the second proposition was divided in two parts (renumbered as 'I lim. 1 [*old number*]' and 'II lim.'), while the second limitation to the second proposition was renumbered as the first limitation to the third proposition ('I. lim. III. prop. 2 [*old number*]'). The original numbering is indicated by square brackets. Grotius addresses the third proposition in the next part of his treatise.

4 First Grotius wrote: 'Maiorem charitatem erga fideles quam erga Infideles demonstrandam'.

5 Perhaps Grotius wrote 'inde'.

6 This phrase ('II. Lim[itatio] … ex 2 P[raemissio]ne') has later been added in the margin. It interrupts Grotius's original argument. The phrase 'Quo forte … seq[uentia]' can also be read as a continuation of the first limitation ('Maior charitas … domesticos fidei').

is set before you. 1Cor. 10.27.[1] Objection: Deut. 5 and the added reason.[2] This, too, is against the institutions of the Jews, who blamed Christ for that reason that he attended banquets with men who were strangers to the Church.[3] It also holds for trade. Abraham and Jacob bought lands from the non-believers.[4] And countless other examples are at hand: although even in this respect some of the Jews seem not to have judged correctly, from which it is believed that the error was born of the disciples, who interpreted Christ's warning about being careful of leaven as if they were forbidden to purchase bread from people of Pharisaic superstition.[5]

The idea of this proposition should be restricted by these additions.

I. Limitation. 1 [*old number*]. Greater charity must be shown towards the faithful than towards the unfaithful. Paul to Gal. 6.10.[6] Let us be charitable to all, but especially to those who are of the household of faith.[7]

II. Limitation. Unless it appears that damage to the faith would result from this; from the second premise. To which perhaps also pertains this rule of the old law: You shall lend to a stranger at usury; but not to your brother.[8] You shall demand [usury] from a foreigner, Deut. 15.3.[9] Now the reason is clear, because in these things, the fellowship of nature is supplemented by the community of

---

1 Grotius quoted the Vulgate text.

2 The connection with the fifth chapter of Deuteronomy, containing the text of the Ten Commandments, is not clear. Perhaps Grotius had Deuteronomy 5.30–31 in mind. These two verses refer to the 'commands, decrees and laws' that the Israelites should abide with, once they had settled in the promised land.

3 See for example Math. 9.9–13; Marc. 2.13–17; Luc. 5.27–32.

4 Gen. 23.1–20; 33.19; Act. 7.16.

5 Cf. Math. 16:5–12.

6 A similar reference to Paulus can be found in Grotius's *Remonstrantie*, where he explains that '[w]hen the apostle Paul enjoins us to be good to all people, in particular our fellow believers, he does presume a closer bond between believers, but does not exclude the unbelievers from the bond of love'. See *Remonstrantie*, fol. 6^{v}, pp. 80–81, trans., p. 202. See also *IBP*, II.15.10.2 (ed. Feenstra, p. 400, n. 1).

7 The quotation, Gal. 6.10, seems to be taken from the Bible translation by Immanuel Tremellius and Franciscus Junius, *Testamenti Veteris Biblia Sacra* (Frankfurt am Main: Ex officina typographica And. Wechelii, 1577–1579), or a later edition: the phrasing is identical. Grotius made use of the edition Hanau: typis Wechelianis, apud Claudium Marnium et haeredes Joannis Aubrii, 1603. Cf. Henk Nellen, *Hugo Grotius: A Lifelong Struggle for Peace in Church and State, 1583–1645* (Leiden: Brill, 2014), p. 635.

8 Deut. 23.19–20. Grotius quotes the translation by Tremellius and Junius (Deut. 23.20).

9 Grotius quotes the translation by Tremellius and Junius.

est colligatio, eo beneficia esse maiora debere ratio dictat. Iam quae v[ide] p[er] seq[uentia].[1]

I. Lim [itatio]. III. Prop[ositio]. 2 [*old number*]. Similiter maior amicitia ac familiaritas cum fidelib[us] quam cum Infidelibus coli debet. Maximum enim amicitiae vinculum est studiorum consensio, praecipue circa res maximas. Hinc illa φιλαδελφία toties in Evangelio commendata. Arist[oteles].

315v 1 praem[issum/issio] in p[ropositione]m.[2]

In p[ropositione]m. Notandum et hic duplices esse Infideles sive ἑτεροδόξους; alios, qui ad Ecclesiam nunquam pertinuerunt; alios qui ab ea desciverunt, aut iudicio Ecclesiastico eiecti sunt. Probatur haec distinctio 1 Cor. 5 v. 12.

II. Lim[itatio]. III. Prop[ositio]. Qui ab Ecclesia defecerunt, aut eius iudicio condemnati sunt, ab horum familiari convictu et consuetudine abstinere[3] Christiani debent: quia hoc ob rationem specialem ita constitutum est, ut ad pudorem et paenitentiam reverentur.[4] Inde haereticum hominem post unam et alteram admonitionem vitari[5] Apostolus praecipit ad Tit. 3.10. Hoc tamen abstinendi praeceptum non ita destrictum est ut necessitatis casum, aut etiam utilitatem omnem excludat, cum sine dubio liceat Fidelib[us] interdum et hos spe conversionis accedere.

Sed et ab aliorum Infidelium consuetudine abstinere iis saltem expedit qui infirmitatis suae sunt conscii.[6]

III. Lim[itatio] ex III p[rae]m[isso/issione].[7] Non admodum arcta familiaritas cum Infid[elibus] et Haer[eticis] sine causa ineunda, sed qui cum alterius

1 The reading of this phrase is not completely certain.

2 The reading is uncertain. Perhaps these cryptic notes are just a reminder that does not belong to the text.

3 Grotius marked 'abstinere' with a sign to indicate that after this word the sentence beginning with the words 'Hoc tamen abstinendi …' should follow.

4 'reverentur' seems an error. Peter Borschberg, 'De societate', p. 375, n. 102, reads: 'revertentur'; a plausible alternative is: 'revertantur' or 'reveniant', third-person plural present subjunctive of 'revertor' and 'revenio' (I return).

5 After the word 'vitari' Grotius deleted: 'debere'.

6 Grotius deleted this sentence by placing two diagonal lines.

7 Or should we read: 'ex III p[ropositio]ne'?

grace. Reason dictates that the closer the connection, the greater the benefits should be. Now see what follows.

I. Limitation. III. Proposition. 2 [*old number*]. Likewise greater friendship and familiarity should be cultivated with the faithful than with the non-believers. For the greatest bond of friendship is the harmony of strivings, especially concerning the greatest matters.[1] Hence that brotherly love (φιλαδελφία) is so often recommended in the Gospel.[2] Aristotle.[3]

315v First premise to the proposition.

To the proposition. It should also be noted here that there are two kinds of non-believers or ἑτεροδόξοι; those who never belonged to the Church; and those who departed from it, or are expelled by an ecclesiastical judgement. This distinction is approved in 1 Cor. 5 v. 12.[4]

II. Limitation. III. Proposition. Christians must abstain from intimate relations and social intercourse with those who have fallen from the Church, or have been condemned by its judgement: because this is so arranged for a special reason, that they should return to shame and repentance. Hence the Apostle to Tit. 3.10 commands to avoid a heretical man after one admonition and another. However, this precept of abstinence is not so restricted as to exclude the case of necessity, or even all utility, since it is without doubt permissible for the faithful to sometimes approach these heretics with the hope of conversion.

But it is at least expedient for those who are aware of their weakness to abstain from the intercourse with other non-believers.

III. Limitation from the third premise. It is recommended not to enter into a very close familiarity with non-believers and heretics without reason, but those who converse with non-believers of another kind should take care on

1 Cf. Cic. *Planc.* 2.5; Cic. *Amic.* 4.15.

2 See for instance Rom. 12.10; Hebr. 13.1; 1 Thess. 4.9.

3 Cf. Aristot. *et. Nic.* 1156b, 1157a and 1158ab. See also *IBP*, II.15.10.2 (ed. Feenstra, p. 400), with a reference to Aristot. *et. Nic.* 1126b27.

4 Cf. the reference to 1 Cor. 5 in *IPC*, ed. Hamaker, p. 211, n. 3. Vitoria had also evoked 1 Cor. 5 to assert that the Pope has no spiritual or temporal jurisdictions over the infidels (*De Indis*, q. 2, a. 2, § 27). Grotius may have borrowed these references from Vitoria. See also Borschberg, 'De societate', p. 369, n. 64.

generis Infidelibus[1] conversantur diligenter omnibus occasionibus invigilare debent, ut ipsos et doctrina et exemplo conentur ad sanam mentem perducere. 1 Thess. 4.12.

Iam quae societatis genera inter Fideles et Infideles esse possint videamus, tum privatim, tum publice, nam in utroque ferme eadem est ratio. Ac primum videamus in societate aequali; cuius diversi sunt gradus.
Primum gradum aequalem ponamus convictum et familiaritatem.

III. Prop[ositio]. Licet amicitiam aliquam et familiaritatem cum Infid[elibus] et cum Haer[eticis] habere. Ex sup[eriore loco].[2]

IV. Prop[ositio]. Summa coniunctio est in matrimonio. Agitur autem aut de contracto aut de contrahendo. Contracto non licet ab Infideli divertere. 1 Cor. 7.12.

Lim[itatio]. Quod tamen ita puto intelligendum, ut liceat Magistratui fideli ferre legem qua matrimonium fidelis cum Infideli nullum et irritum declaretur ita ut non obliget. Est enim in[3] Magistratus potestate ob iustas causas contractus[4] irritos facere. Talis lex cum apud Iudaeos fuerit, recte Esdras tempore αὐτονομίας Iudaeos ab Infidelium contubernio iussit discedere. [Esdras] c[ap.] 10.

V. Prop[ositio]. Si de contrahendo agatur in universum non possunt non damnari matrimonia cum Infidelibus: quia qui praecipuus est finis matrimonii educatio liberorum ad gloriam Dei in[5] tali coniugio non parum impeditur.[6] Ita ut locum hic suum habeat: illud nolite iugum ducere, ἑτεροζυγεῖν, cum Infidelibus.

1 After 'Infidelibus' Grotius deleted three illegible characters, possibly 'fam'.
2 Or: 'ex sup[positione]'.
3 'in' added above the line.
4 After 'contractus' Grotius deleted: 'aliquos'.
5 'in' is possibly deleted.
6 Instead of 'non parum impeditur' Grotius initially wrote: 'non satis respicitur'.

all occasions, so that they try to bring them to good sense both by doctrine and example. 1Thess. 4.12.

Now let us see what kinds of partnership there can be between believers and non-believers, both privately and publicly, for in both cases the principle is almost the same. And let us first consider an equal partnership; of which there are different degrees.
Let us point out that the first degree [comprises of] living together and familiarity on an equal footing.

III. Proposition. It is permissible to have some friendship and familiarity with non-believers and with heretics. From [above].

IV. Proposition. The highest union is in marriage. Now it is a matter of either a concluded marriage or a marriage to be concluded. In case of a concluded marriage it is not permissible to separate from the non-believer. 1Cor. 7.12.[1]

Limitation. However, I think that it should be understood in such a way that it is permissible for a faithful magistrate to make a law by which the marriage of a faithful person with an unbeliever is declared null and void, so that it does not bind. For it is in the power of the magistrate to invalidate contracts for just reasons. Because such a law existed among the Jews, Ezra rightly commanded the Jews at the time of independence (αὐτονομία) to depart from the common dwelling with the non-believers. [Ezra] c[hapter] 10.[2]

V. Proposition. If it is a question of contracting in general it is impossible not to condemn marriages with non-believers: because the main purpose of marriage, the education of children to the glory of God, is in such a union not a little hindered. So that it has its place here: do not yoke, ἑτεροζυγεῖν, with the

---

1 Cf. the reference to 1Cor. 7.12 in Grotius, *Remonstrantie*, fol. 28 [=29]^{v} (ad art. 36), p. 172–173, trans., p. 213, where Grotius writes: 'The Apostle Paul, speaking of this matter, advises a believer who is married to an unbeliever not to divorce if the unbeliever wants to continue to live together.'

2 Cf. the reference to Ezra 10 in Grotius, *Remonstrantie*, fol. 28 [=29]^{v} (ad art. 36), p. 172–173, trans. p. 213, where Grotius writes: 'Whether a city government might be allowed to end such a marriage by public order might be contested, in light of the example of Ezra, who commanded it, and the opinion of Augustine and some others, who believe that such a thing is allowed.'

2 Cor. 6.13 [= 14]. Sc[aliger], Anim[adversiones] in Euseb[ium], 149. Solomon hoc nomine reprehenditur et Manassis frater summi pontificis dicitur sacerdotium tali coniugio polluisse. Neh. 13 v. 26 et 28.

Lim[itatio]. Excipe eos qui ad hoc vocantur specialiter, quod forte de Esthera dici potest. An idem obtineat in casu necessitatis, puta si quis continentiae dono non praeditus eo loco sit ut aliter uxorem habere non possit, consideratione indiget; nisi quod haud impie credetur Deum providere, ne sui fideles ad eas angustias coarctentur. Hic eius subiectio. De affinitate. Deut. 7.

317r His similia in publicis societatibus procedunt.

Concl[usio] II. Nam foedera cum Infidelibus amicitiae,[1] commerciorum, itinerum aliorumque beneficiorum quae mutuo praestantur causa recte ineuntur. Tale foedus Solomonis cum Hiramo fuit 1 Reg. 5.11 et 10.22. Igitur quod simile foedus in Iosaphato reprehenditur, ex iis quae VI loco praemissa sunt interpretationem recipit. 2 Chr. 20.37.

Limit[atio]. Nisi hoc forte eam rationem habet specialem,[2] quia Rex Isr[ael] erat apostata.

Restringe: ita haec fieri debere ut interim Fidelibus non minora beneficia aut etiam maiora praestentur.

In praemiss[a]. Ad societatem bellicam quod attinet, ea duplex est: ἐπιμαχία et συμμαχία, hoc est, defensiva et offensiva. Utraque sive cum Infidelibus sive

1 'amicitiae' placed above the line.

2 Perhaps Grotius changed this passage in: 'Nisi hoc forte ea ratione speciali …'.

non-believers. 2 Cor. 6.13 [= 14].[1] Scaliger, Animadversiones in Eusebium, 149.[2] Solomon is reproached for this reason, and Manassis, the brother of the high priest, is said to have defiled the priesthood with such a marriage. Neh. 13 v. 26 and 28.[3]

Limitation. Make an exception for those who are especially called to this, which may perhaps be said of Esther. Whether the same pertains in a case of necessity, for example, if a person, not endowed with the gift of self-restraint, finds himself in such a place where he cannot otherwise have a wife, needs consideration; except that it is by no means impious to believe that God will provide that his faithful should not be constrained to such straits. Here is her submission.[4] On kinship. Deut. 7.

317r These same things occur in public alliances.

Conclusion II. For treaties with the non-believers are rightly entered into for the sake of friendship, commerce, travels, and other benefits which are mutually guaranteed. Such was Solomon's treaty with Hiram, 1 Reg. 5.11 and 10.22.[5] Therefore, the fact that a similar treaty is criticized in Jehoshaphat receives an interpretation from what is stated in the sixth premise. 2 Chr. 20.37.[6]

Limitation. Unless perhaps this has a special reason, because the king of Israel was an apostate.

Make a restriction: these things must be done in such a way that in the meantime the faithful are not given less but even greater benefits.

Regarding the premises. As regards a military alliance, it is of two types: ἐπιμαχία and συμμαχία,[7] that is, defensive and offensive. [An alliance] entered into

1 Grotius quoted the Vulgate text.

2 See Josephus Justus Scaliger, *Thesaurus temporum* (Lugduni Batavorum: Excudebat Basson et Commelinus, 1606), with a separately paginated *Animadversiones in Chronologica Eusebii*. See Molhuysen, 'De bibliotheek van Hugo de Groot', no. 26. On this place in the *Animadversiones* Scaliger discussed the ancestry of king Herod the Great (c. 72 BCE–c. 4 BCE), son of a Jewish father and an Arab mother.

3 See also reading notes, fol. 316 (2)v.

4 This remark is unclear and relates perhaps to Esther (underlined in the text).

5 See also 1 Reg. 5.26; 9.10–14; 2 Chr. 8.17–18 and 9.10–11.

6 Cf. *IBP*, II.15.9.7 (ed. Feenstra, p. 398).

7 The same distinction is made in *IPC*, ed. Hamaker, p. 65, n. 5, ed. Van Ittersum, p. 100, n. c, with a reference to Thuc. 1.44 and the Scholiast thereon, and in *IBP*, II.15.6.3, with a reference to Zosimus, liber 5 [42] (ed. Feenstra, p. 393, n. 6).

cum Fidelibus inita iniusta est, si in omne futurum bellum contrahitur,[1] sine exceptione, nisi causa[2] iniusta sit.[3]

Concl[usio] III. In bello autem iusto Infideles[4] recte a Fidelibus defendentur, etiamsi ii qui Infideles opprimunt Fideles haberi velint. Imo hoc opus non modo licitum, sed et summe laudabile et ex circumstantiis saepe necessarium est; ex 2 Prop[ositione]. Ps. 82.4; Prov. 24.1.

Limit[atio]. Excipe, nisi revelatum sit Deum aliquas[5] gentes ob Infidelitatem velle punire. Inde illud: osores Iehovae diligere te. 2 Chr. 19.2. Item: Non enim est Iehova cum Israelitis. 2 Chr. 25.7.

Concl[usio] IV. Vicissim fideles bellum iustum gerentes auxilio Infidelium uti possunt.[6] A quib[us][7] accipienda beneficia. Sen[eca] 2 [De] Ben[eficiis] 18.

1. Dum ne occasio ea ratione detur Infidelib[us] nocendi veritati.
2. Dum ne fiat ex diffidentia.

Aut contra praeceptum speciale: ut Iud[aei] in accersendis Aegyptiorum auxiliis.

Concl[usio] V. Summa publica societas est unio reipublicae. Quin[8] autem populus fidelis cum infideli in una[9] republica manere possit dubium non est.
Sc[aliger] in Anim[adversionibus] ad Eus[ebium] 148.
Exemplum: Iud[aei] cum Idum[aeis]; Israel[ites] cum Aegypt[iis].

Concl[usio] VI. An autem sponte in talem communionem venire debeat, plus habet difficultatis. Cumque hoc matrimonio non sit dissimile, et fini verae rei-

1 Perhaps read: 'contrahatur'.
2 'causa': Grotius first wrote 'causae', followed by a deleted word: 'iustae'.
3 The reasoning is unclear. Perhaps Grotius intended to write: '… nisi causa iusta sit'.
4 After 'Infideles' Grotius deleted: 'oppressi'.
5 Grotius corrected the word 'aliquas' from: 'tales'.
6 Instead of 'uti possunt' Grotius first wrote: 'utuntur'.
7 Reading uncertain. A less probable alternative is: 'A quol[ibet]'.
8 'Quin': written in the margin. In the text Grotius deleted the variant 'an'.
9 Grotius first wrote 'unam'.

either with the non-believers or with the faithful, is unjust if war is agreed to for every future, without exception, unless the cause is just.

Conclusion III. But in a just war the non-believers will be rightly defended by the faithful, even if those who oppress the non-believers wish to be considered as faithful. Nay, this work is not only permitted, but also highly praiseworthy, and because of the circumstances often necessary; from the second proposition. Ps. 82.4; Prov. 24.1.[1]

Limitation. Make an exception, unless it has been revealed that God wants to punish some nations for infidelity. Hence the saying: should you love those who hated Jehovah. 2 Chr. 19.2. Again: For Jehovah is not with the Israelites. 2 Chr. 25.7.[2]

Conclusion IV. On the other hand, the faithful who are waging a just war can use the help of the non-believers. From whom benefits are to be received. Seneca in 2 *On Benefits* 18.

1. As long as no occasion is thereby offered to the non-believers for harming the truth.
2. As long as it is not done out of distrust.

Or against a special command: as the Jews in calling for the Egyptian auxiliaries.[3]

Conclusion V. The highest public partnership is the union of the state. But there is no doubt that a faithful people can remain in one state with non-believers. Scaliger in Animadversionibus ad Eusebium 148.[4]
Example: Jews with Idumeans; Israelites with Egyptians.

Conclusion VI. But whether a people should voluntarily enter into such a communion is more difficult. And since this is not unlike marriage, and not a little

1 Cf. *IBP*, II.15.9.10 (ed. Feenstra, p. 399, n. 9).

2 Cf. *IBP*, II.15.9.7 (ed. Feenstra, p. 398, n. 2 [= 3] and 7). Grotius quoted 2 Chr. 19.2 and 25.7 from the translation by Tremellius and Junius.

3 See for example Esa. 30.2–3 and 31.1–3. Cf. *IBP*, II.15.9.9 (ed. Feenstra, p. 399, n. 6).

4 See above, p. 95, n. 2 on Scaliger's *Thesaurus*. On pp. 148–149 of the *Animadversiones in Chronologica Eusebii*, a separately paginated part of the *Thesaurus*, Scaliger explains how the Judaeans commingled with the Idumaeans at the time of the Maccabean leader John Hyrcanus (164 BCE–104 BCE).

publicae non parum repugnet, idem docendum videtur, maxime extra casum necessitatis, et cum Infidelibus qui ab Ecclesia abierunt.
Societas inaequalis aut Fideles superiores aut inferiores facit; estque aut privata aut publica. 1 Reg. 5.6.

Prop[ositio] VI. Fidelibus licet habere ministros atque etiam servos infideles. Th[omas] 2. 2. 10. 9.

317v Concl[usio]. VII. Pariter Magistratui aut Populo Fideli licet populum Infidelem in ditionem suam accipere.

Prop[ositio] VII. Licet Fideli operam suam locare Infideli. Esdras. Nehemias. Iosephus. Daniel. Vide[1] Philipp. 4.22.

Prop[ositio] VIII. Fidelis si sit servus Infidelis domini[2] talis manere debet. 1 ad Tim. 6.1. Potest tamen fidelis Magistratus lege lata Dominium Infidelium in homines fideles in ditionib[us] suis impedire, quae lex iustam habet rationem. C. ne Christ. manc. L. unica.

Prop[ositio] IX. Sponte autem dare se in servitutem ne Fideli quidem extra casum necessitatis facile licet. Infideli multo minus. Tamen in casu necessitatis non videtur prohibitum.

Concl[usio] VIII. Pariter populo fideli[3] incumbit obsequi Principi aut Magistratui Infideli. Lex tamen fieri potest in Rep[ublica] ut Princeps factus[4] Infidel[is] principatu excidat.

Concl[usio] IX. At tali se subiicere, vix licet. 1 Cor. 6.1 et 6. Deut. 17.15: e Fratri[bus] tuis.

1 Reading uncertain.
2 'domini' added above the line.
3 After 'fideli' Grotius deleted three words: 'non licet', and an illegible word, possibly 'inire'.
4 Reading not completely certain.

inconsistent with the end of a true state, it seems that the same thing should be taught, especially outside cases of necessity, and with non-believers who have departed from the Church.
An unequal partnership either makes the faithful superior or inferior; and it is either private or public. 1Reg. 5.6.[1]

Proposition VI. It is permissible for the faithful to have non-believers as servants and even as slaves. Thomas 2. 2. 10. 9.

317v Conclusion. VII. It is equally permissible for a faithful magistrate or people to accept an infidel people under its authority.

Proposition VII. It is permissible for the faithful to lend his services to the faithless. Ezra, Nehemiah, Joseph, Daniel.[2] See Philipp. 4.22

Proposition VIII. If a faithful [slave] is a slave of an unfaithful master, he must remain so. 1 to Tim. 6.1. It is possible, however, for a faithful magistrate, by law, to prevent the ownership of non-believers over faithful men under his jurisdiction, which law has a just reason. C. ne Christ. manc. L. unica.[3]

Proposition IX. But it is not easily allowed to submit oneself voluntarily in servitude to a believer, except in cases of necessity. Much less so to a non-believer. However, in case of necessity, it does not seem to be prohibited.

Conclusion VIII. Likewise, it is incumbent upon a faithful people to obey an infidel prince or magistrate. However, a law can be made in the state so that a prince who has become unfaithful may be deposed from his leadership.

Conclusion IX. But it is hardly permissible to submit oneself to such a prince. 1Cor. 6.1 and 6. Deut. 17.15: from your brothers.[4]

---

1 See 1Reg. 5.6: 'Praecipe igitur ut praecidant mihi servi tui cedros de Libano, et servi mei sint cum servis tuis'.

2 See for instance Ezra 6.8; Neh. 2.8–9; Gen. 39.4; 41.39–57; Dan. 1.4. Ezra and Nehemiah rebuilt the temple and wall in Jerusalem under the auspices of the Persian king. Potiphar, captain of the Pharaoh's guard, made Joseph master of his household. Daniel and his companions held important positions at the Babylonian court.

3 See *Cod.* 1.10.1–2 and *Cod. Th.* 16.9: 'Ne Christianum mancipium iudaeus habeat'. Cf. the reference to this law in Grotius, *Remonstrantie*, fol. 27[=28]v, p. 166–167, trans., p. 213.

4 Deut. 17.15: '… eum [regem] constitues, quem Dominus Deus tuus elegerit de numero fratrum tuorum'.

Ampl[ificatio].[1] Distingue: ut minus liceat Apostatae se subiicere quam tantum Infideli.

Lim[itatio]. Deinde, ut in protectionem se dare Infideli salva religione et libertate aliqua non videatur prohibitum. Ita Iacobus se Regis Aegyptii fidei permisit. Rex Solomon civitates aliquas Hiramo tributarias fecit.

Lim[itatio]. Praeterea ut liceat etiam sine exceptione se Infideli subiicere ubi est speciale Dei imperium: ut Iudaei Assyrio iussi sunt se mancipare. Ierem. 27.8.

Lim[itatio]. Idem probabiliter dici posset in ultimo casu necessitatis, arg[umentum] Ierem. 27.13.

David Israelitis pepercit.[2]

1 'Ampl[ificatio]': corrected from: 'Lim[itatio]'.

2 These three words hastily added by Grotius in a later hand.

Amplification. Note the distinction: that it is less permissible to submit oneself to an apostate than just to a non-believer.

Limitation. Then, it does not seem to be forbidden to place oneself under the protection of an infidel, in order to save religion and some freedom. Thus Jacob committed himself to the good faith of the king of Egypt.[1] King Solomon made certain cities tributary to Hiram.[2]

Limitation. Moreover, that it is permissible even without exception to submit oneself to a non-believer where there is a special command of God: as the Jews were ordered to subject themselves to Assyria. Ierem. 27.8.

Limitation. The same could probably be said in the utmost case of necessity, the argument of Ierem. 27.13.

David spared the Israelites.[3]

---

1 See Gen. 46.1–34; 47.1–12.

2 1 Reg. 9.12; see Grotius's reading notes on fol. 316 (1)^{r}, left column.

3 See 1 Sam. 25.33 and 2 Sam. 5.3.

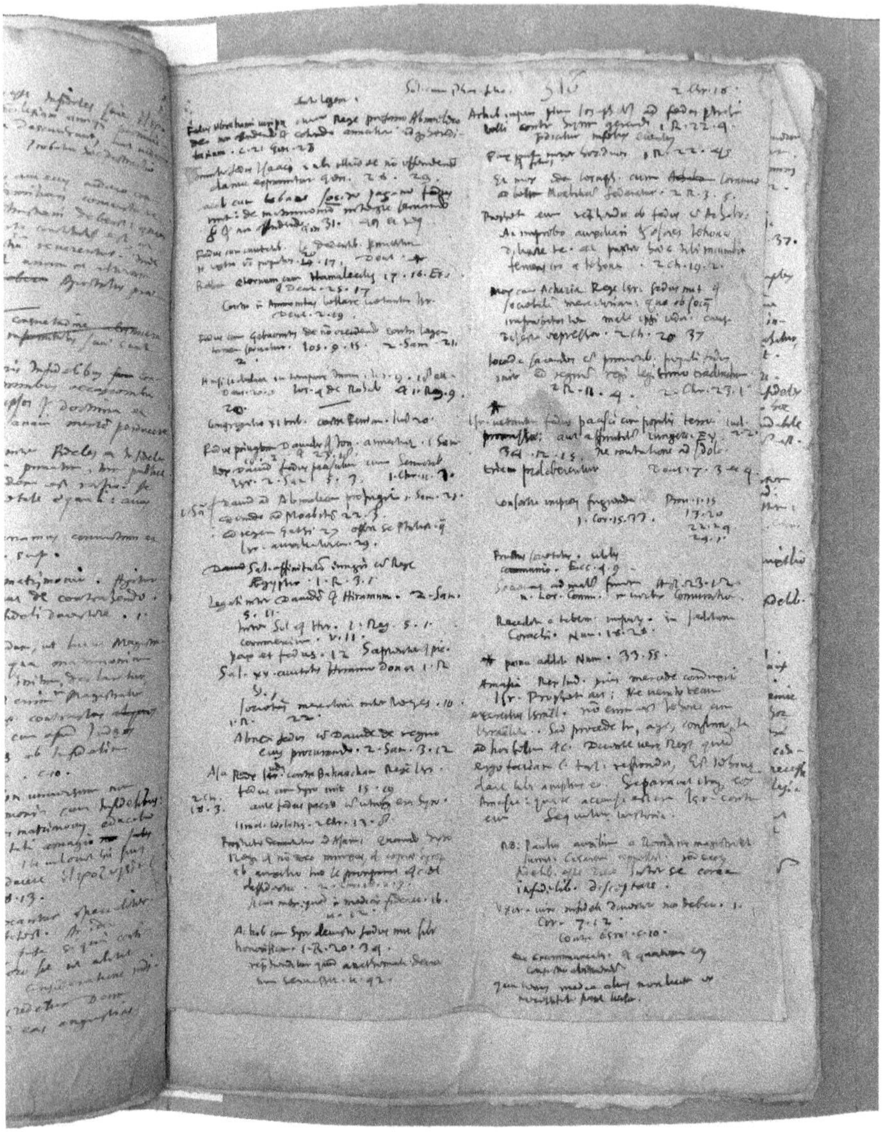

FIGURE 3 Reading notes in *De societate publica cum infidelibus*, written in the hand of Grotius. Leiden University Library, MS BPL 922 IE, fol. 316 (1)^{r}.

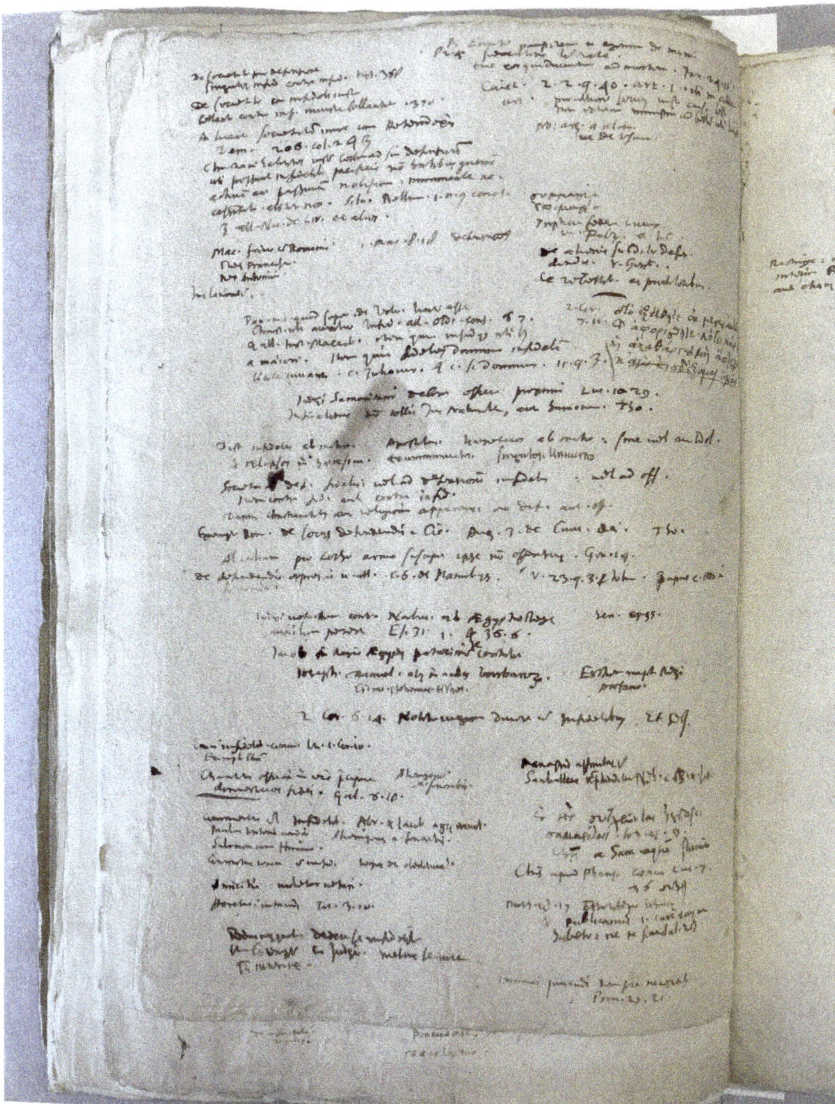

FIGURE 4 Reading notes in *De societate publica cum infidelibus*, written in the hand of Grotius. Leiden University Library, MS BPL 922 IE, fol. 316 (2)ᵛ.

Reading Notes and Source-References

Fol. 316 (1)^{rv}, 316 (2)^{rv} are inserted between fol. 315^{v} and fol. 317^{r}

316 (1)^{r} ***Left column***
Sol[omon] cum Phar[aonis] filia.

Ante legem.

Foedus Abrahami viri pii cum Rege profano Abimeleco de non offendendo et colenda amicitia idque haereditarium. C[ap.] 21 Gen. 27.

Simile foedus Isaaci: ubi illud de non offendendo clarius exprimitur. Gen. 26.29.

Iacob cum Labane socero pagano foedus init: de matrimonio integre servando, item[1] et non offendendo. Gen. 31.49 et seq[uentes].

Foedus cum civitatib[us] se dedentib[us] permittitur.
Ita:[2] Extra VI populos, 20.17, Deut. *[3]

Bellum aeternum cum Hamalecitis 17. 16, Exo. et Deut. 25.17.

Contra in Ammonitas bellare vetantur Isr[aelites]. Deut. 2.19.

Foedus cum Gabaonitis de non occidendo contra legem tamen servatur. Ios. 9.15; 2 Sam. 21.2.

Ita:[4] nisi se dedunt in tempora Innum[eralia].[5] Ios. 9.18, aliter[6] Deut. 20.10. Ios. et de Rahab et 1 Reg. 9.20.

Congregatio XI trib[uum] contra Beniam[in]. Iud. 20[.30].

---

1 The meaning of Grotius's scribble is unclear. Perhaps we should read: 'simul'.
2 'Ita': the reading is unclear. Is this a reference sign? Perhaps: 'Item'.
3 First Grotius wrote: '19.27, Deut. *' The meaning of the asterisks in this document is not clear.
4 See above, p. 104, n. 2.
5 'Innum[era]', 'Innum[erabilia]' or 'Innum[eralia]'.
6 'aliter': reading uncertain. Perhaps we should read: 'aut'. In *IPC* we often find: 'all'.

16 (1)r *Left column*
Solomon with Pharaoh's daughter.

Before the Law.[1]

The pact of Abraham, the pious man, with the heathen king Abimelech, of non-offensiveness and of cultivating friendship, and that was hereditary. C[hapter] 21 Gen. 27.[2]

A similar pact of Isaac: where the pact of non-offensiveness is more clearly expressed. Gen. 26.29.

Jacob enters into a pact with his heathen father-in-law Laban: of keeping the marriage intact and of non-offensiveness. Gen. 31.49 and following.[3]

A pact with surrendering peoples is allowed.
That is: except for the six peoples, 20.17, Deut. *

Eternal war with the Amalekites 17.16. Ex. and Deut. 25.17.[4]

On the other hand, the Israelites are forbidden to make war on the Ammonites. Deut. 2.19.[5]

The pact with the Gibeonites about not killing is still kept against the law. Ios. 9.15; 2 Sam. 21.2.

That is: unless they give themselves up forever. Ios. 9.18. otherwise Deut. 20.10. Ios. and about Rahab[6] and 1 Reg. 9.20.

The gathering of the eleven tribes against Benjamin. Iud. 20[.30].[7]

---

1 The reference ('Ante legem') is to the four eras of men that are distinguished in Christian theology since the Middle Ages: *ante legem* (i.e. the Mosaic law), *sub lege*, *sub gratia* (i.e. the redemption by Christ's death) and *sub pace* (i.e. after the final judgement), see Aug. *Exp. Ep. ad Romanos* 13–18; *Exp. Ep. ad Galatas* 46.—ed. J. Divjak 1971, CSEL 84 Augustinus.
2 See Gen. 21.27. Cf. Gen. 20 and 26 on another Abimelech, probably a son.
3 Cf. the reference to the treaty between Jacob and Laban in *IBP*, II.15.9.1 (ed. Feenstra, p. 395).
4 Cf. *IBP*, II.15.9.1 (ed. Feenstra, p. 395).
5 Cf. *IBP*, II.15.9.4 (ed. Feenstra, p. 397).
6 Cf. Ios. 2.1–6; 2.12–14; 6.17, 23 and 25.
7 See also Iud. 20.10.

Foedus privatim Davidis et Ion[athae] amicitiae. 1 Sam. 18.2 et 23.18.
Rex David foedus paciscitur cum seniorib[us] Isr[ael]. 2 Sam. 5.3; 1 Chr. 11.3.

1 Sam. David ad Abimelecum profugit. 1 Sam. 21.
Deinde ad Moabitos. [1 Sam.] 22.3.
Ad regem Gathi, [1 Sam.] 27, offert se Philist[iim] q[uam] Isr[ael] auxiliatorem. [1 Sam.] 29.

Sal[omon][1] affinitatem iungit cum Rege Aegyptio. 1 R[eg.] 3.1.

Legati inter Davidem et Hiramum. 2 Sam. 5.11.
Inter Sol[omon] et Hir[amum]. 1 Reg. 5.1;
commercium, v. 11;
pax et foedus, [v.] 12. Sapienter et pie.

Sal[omon] XX civitates Hiramo donat. 1 R[eg.] 9.12
Societas mercatoria inter Reges. 10. 1 R[eg.] 22.
Abneri foedus cum Davide de regno eius procurando. 2 Sam. 3.12

Asa Rex Iudae[2] contra Bahascham Regem Isr[ael] foedus cum Syro init. [1 Reg.] 15.19.
Ante foedus pacis[3] (2 Chr. 16.3) cum utroque erat[4] Syro.
Israel. Idolatria. 2 Chr. 13.8.

Prophetae denuntiatio ad Asam: quando Syro Regi et non Deo innixus, et copiae Syrorum ab auxilio tuo se proripiunt etc. de diffidentia. 2 Chr. 16. v. 7.
Sicut infra: quod in medicis fideret. [2 Chr.] 16. v. 12.

---

1 'Sal[omon]': corrected from: 'David'.
2 First Grotius wrote: 'Isr[ael]'.
3 After 'pacis' Grotius inserted a sign that probably refers to a proof-text (2 Chr. 16.3) placed in the left margin.
4 Reading not completely certain.

A pact of friendship concluded privately between David and Jonathan. 1Sam. 18.2 and 23.18.
King David makes a treaty with the elders of Israel. 2Sam. 5.3; 1Chr. 11.3.

1Sam. David fled to Abimelech. 1Sam. 21.
Then to the Moabites. [1Sam.] 22.3.
To the king of Gath, [1Sam.] 27, he offers himself as an auxiliary from Israel to the Philistines. [1Sam.] 29.

Solomon makes an alliance by marriage with the king of Egypt. 1Reg. 3.1.

Ambassadors between David and Hiram. 2Sam. 5.11.
Between Solomon and Hiram 1Reg. 5.1;
trade, verse 11.
peace and pact, [verse] 12. Wisely and piously.[1]

Salomon gives twenty cities to Hiram. 1Reg. 9.12.
A partnership for trade between the kings. 10.1Reg. 22.[2]
A pact with David made by Abner concerning the procuration of the latter's kingdom. 2Sam. 3.12.

Asa king of Judah enters into a treaty with Syria against Bahasha, king of Israel. [1Reg.] 15.19.
Before, Syria had a peace treaty (2Chr. 16.3) with both kings.
Israel. Idolatry. 2Chr. 13.8.

The announcement of the prophet to Asa: because you relied on the Syrian king and not on God, the forces of the Syrians also have rushed away from your help, etc. on distrust. 2Chr. 16. v. 7.[3]
As below: that he trusted the doctors. [2Chr.] 16. v. 12.[4]

1 1Reg. 5.1; 5.11 and 5.12: Grotius follows here the verse numbering of the Vulgate. Cf. the reference to the treaties of David and Solomon with Hiram, king of Tyre, in *IBP*, II.15.9.2, ed. Feenstra, p. 396, n. 1 (2Sam. 5.11) and n. 2 (1Reg. 5.12).

2 Probably Grotius refers to 1Reg. 10.22.

3 Grotius quoted from the Bible translation by Immanuel Tremellius and Franciscus Junius. Cf. *IBP*, II.15.9.9 (ed. Feenstra, p. 399).

4 Cf. *IBP*, II.15.9.9 (ed. Feenstra, p. 399).

Achab cum Syro devicto foedus init sibi honorificum. 1 R[eg.] 20.34. Reprehenditur quod anathemate devotum servasset, v. 42.

316 (1)r *Right column*
2 Chr. 16.

Achab impius pium Iosaphatum ad foedus pertrahit belli contra Syrum gerendi. 1 R[eg.] 22.4. Praedicitur infelix eventum.

Pax inita inter hos duos, 1 R[eg.] 22.45; et filios.

Et mox idem Iosaph[atus] cum[1] Ioramio[2] ad bellum Moabiticum foederatur. 2 R[eg.] 3.5.

Propheta eum reprehendit ob foedus cum Achabo:
An improbo auxiliari et osores Iehovae diligere te [oportuit]? At propter haec tibi incumbit fervens ira a Iehova. 2 Ch[r]. 19.2.

Mox cum Achazia Rege Isr[ael] foedus init et societatem mercatoriam: quae ob socii improbitatem male ipsi cedit, causa diserte expressa. 2 Ch[r]. 20.37.

Ioiada sacerdos cum primorib[us] populi foedus init ad regnum regi legitimo tradendum.
2 R[eg.] 11.4; 2 Chr. 23.1.

*

Isr[aelitae] vetantur foedus pacisci cum populis terrae promissae; aut affinitatem iungere. Ex. 34.12 [et] 15; ne mutatione ad Idolatriam prolaberentur. Deut. 7.3 et 4. Iud. 2.2.

Consortia impiorum fugienda. 1 Cor. 15.33. Prov. 1.15; 13.20; 22.24; 24.1.

Fructus societatis. Utilis communio. Ecc. 4.9.

1 After 'cum' Grotius deleted: 'Achabo'.
2 'Ioramio': read 'Ioram' or 'Ioramo'.

Ahab enters into an honorable treaty with conquered Syria. 1 Reg. 20.34. He is blamed for having spared someone struck with a curse, v. 42.[1]

16 (1)r *Right column*
2 Chr. 16.

The impious Ahab draws the pious Jehoshaphat into a treaty to wage war against Syria. 1 Reg. 22.4. An unfortunate ending is foretold.

Peace was made between these two, 1 Reg. 22.45; and [their] sons.

And soon the same Jehoshaphat is bound in an alliance with Jehoram for the Moabite war. 2 Reg. 3.5.

The prophet reproached him for his pact with Ahab:
Did you have to help a depraved man and love those who hated Jehovah? But because of these things the burning anger of Jehovah lies upon you. 2 Chr. 19.2.[2]

Soon he entered into a treaty and a commercial partnership with Ahaziah, king of Israel: which due to dishonesty of his partner turned out badly for him, for a reason eloquently expressed. 2 Chr. 20.37.

Joiada the priest enters into a covenant with the foremost of the people to hand over the kingdom to the rightful king. 2 Reg. 11.4; 2 Chr. 23.1.

*

The Israelites are forbidden to negotiate a treaty with the peoples of the promised land; or to enter into an alliance of marriage. Ex. 34.12 [and] 15; so that they do not fall into idolatry by the exchange. Deut. 7.3 and 4. Iud. 2.2.

The company of the unfaithful must be avoided. 1 Cor. 15.33. Prov. 1.15; 13.20; 22.24; 24.1.[3]

The fruits of society. A useful companionship. Ecc. 4.9.

---

1 Achab did not abide by God's command to kill Ben-Hadad, king of Aram, 'devoted to destruction'.

2 2 Chr. 19.2 was taken from the Bible translation by Tremellius and Junius. See also, for a reference to 2 Chr. 19.2, *IBP*, II.15.9.7 (ed. Feenstra, p. 398, n. 2 [=3]).

3 Cf. *IBP*, II.15.9 (ed. Feenstra, p. 399), for the last three Bible places in this order.

Societas ad malum finem. Act. 23.12. V[ide] Loc[os] Comm[unes] in verbo Coniuratio.

Recedite a tabern[aculis] impiorum in seditione Corachi. Num. 16.26.

* paena addita Num. 33.55.

Amasia Rex Iud[ae] prius[1] mercede conduxit Isr[aelitas]. Propheta ait: Ne venito tecum exercitus Israel[itarum]. Non enim est Iehova cum Israelitis. Sed procede tu, age, confirma te ad hoc bellum, etc. Dicente vero Rege quid ergo faciam c[entum] tal[entis]? Respondit: Est Iehovae dare tibi amplius eo. Separavit[2] itaque eos Amasia: quare accensa est ira Isr[aelitarum] contra eum. Sequitur victoria.

No[ta]: Paulus auxilium a Romanis magistratib[us] sumit. Caesarem appellat. Indecorum fidelib[us] esse dicit inter se coram infidelib[us] disceptare.

Uxor a viro infideli divertere non debet. 1 Cor. 7.12.
Contra Esrae c[ap.] 10.

De Excommunicatis; et quatenus eorum consortio abstinendum.

1 Perhaps Grotius wrote: 'pius'.
2 'Separavit' in the sense of discharged them (i.e. the troops that had come to him from Ephraim of Israel).

Partnership for a bad aim. Act. 23.12. See Commonplaces on the word 'conspiracy'.[1]

Depart from the camp of the impious in the rebellion of Korah. Num. 16.26.[2]

* penalty added Num. 33.55.

King Amaziah of Judah first hired the Israelites for a fee. The Prophet said: Do not let the army of Israel come with you. For Jehovah is not with the Israelites. But go on, act, strengthen yourself for this war, etc.[3] While the king rightly says, what then shall I do with a hundred talents? He answered: Jehovah is able to give you more than this.[4] Amaziah therefore discharged them: wherefore the anger of the Israelites was kindled against him.[5] Victory follows.

Note: Paul receives help from the Roman authorities. He appeals to the emperor.[6] He says that it is unworthy of the faithful to argue among themselves in the presence of the unfaithful.[7]

A wife should not divorce from an unfaithful husband. 1Cor. 7.12.[8]
Against Ezra c[hapter] 10.[9]

On the excommunicated; and to what extent their company is to be abstained from.

---

1 Grotius's library, confiscated in 1619, included Augustinus Marloratus, *Propheticae et apostolicae, id est totius divinae ac canonicae Scripturae thesaurus in locos communes … digestus*, ed. Guil. Feuguerius (Bern: Ioannes Le Preux, 1601), with the items 'coniuratio' (pp. 176–177) and 'foedus' (pp. 338–339). See Molhuysen, 'De bibliotheek van Hugo de Groot', no. 267. But it is also possible that Grotius cited Josephus Langius, *Loci communes sive florilegium rerum et materiarum selectarum … ex Sacris Litteris …* (Argentorati: Iosias Rihelius, 1605), pp. 122–123, s.v. 'coniuratio', esp. the 'Exempla sacra', with a reference to Act. 23.12.

2 Grotius quoted from the Vulgate text.

3 2Chr. 25.7–8, literally quoted according to the translation by Tremellius and Junius. Cf. *IBP*, II.15.9.7 (ed. Feenstra, p. 398).

4 2Chr. 25.9. The passage differs from the translation by Tremellius and Junius. Here we read: 'Dicente vero Amatzja viro Dei: quid ergo faciendum centum talentis, quae dedi turmae Israelitarum? Dixit vir Dei: est Iehovae dare tibi amplius eo'.

5 The translation of 2Chr. 25.10 in Tremellius and Junius: '… quapropter accensa est ira ipsorum valde contra Jehudam'.

6 Act. 25.25 and 26.32.

7 1Cor. 6.1.

8 Cf. the reference to 1Cor. 7.12 in Grotius, *Remonstrantie*, fol. 28 [=29]v (ad art. 36), p. 172–173.

9 Cf. the reference to Ezra 10 in ibid., fol. 28 [=29]v (ad art. 36), p. 172–173.

Quatenus media alias non licita ex necessitate fiunt licita.

316 (1)[v] *This folio side is left blank.*

316 (2)[r] Eleemosyna an propinquioribus facienda an peccatori[bus].
Quo ordine Th[omas] 2. 2. 32. 9.
Utrum magis diligendi meliores an coniunctiores 2. 2. 26. 7.

316 (2)[v] ***Left column***
De societate pro defensione singulorum infid[elium] contra infid[eles]. Vict[oria] 368.

De societate cum infideli iuste bellante contra inf[idelem] iniuste bellantem. 370.

An liceat societatem inire cum Heterodoxis.
Dem. 206. Col. 2 et 3.

Christiani habentes iustum bellum ad sui defensionem uti possunt infidelib[us] pacificis non ha[ben]tibus guerram activam aut passivam nobiscum;

To what extent otherwise impermissible means become permissible by necessity.

(1)v *This folio side is left blank.*

(2)r Whether alms should be given to those to whom we are more closely related or to sinners.
In which order Thomas 2. 2. 32. 9.[1]
Whether the better or the more closely related are to be preferred 2. 2. 26. 7.[2]

(2)v ***Left column***
On the alliance for the defense of some of the non-believers against the non-believers. Vitoria 368.[3]

On the alliance with a non-believer who is waging a just war against a non-believer who is waging an unjust war. 370.[4]

Whether it is permissible to enter into a partnership with the heterodox.
Dem. 206.[5] Col. 2 and 3.[6]

Christians having a just war for their own defense can use peaceful infidels who have no active or passive war with us; when necessity is pressing, not otherwise.

---

1 *S. Th.* 2 2ae, q. 32, a. 9: 'Quibus sit eleemosyna danda'.
2 *S. Th.* 2 2ae, q. 26, a. 7: 'Utrum plus proximum meliorem, quam magis sibi coniunctum'.
3 Vitoria, *De Indis*, q. 3, a. 5, §15. The page number corresponds with the edition of Vitoria's *Relectiones* printed in Lyon in 1557 (Lugduni: apud Iacobum Boyerium, 1557). Cf. the references to Vitoria, *De Indis*, q. 3, a. 5, §15 in *IBP*, II.15.10, ed. Feenstra, p. 399, n. 10 and in *IPC*, ed. Hamaker, p. 298, n. 3, ed. Van Ittersum, p. 434, n. d. According to Feenstra, Grotius possessed a copy of the *editio princeps* of Vitoria's *Relectiones* of 1557 (*IBP*, ed. Feenstra, p. 941, n. 87).
4 Vitoria, *De Indis*, q. 3, a. 7, §17. Cf. *IBP*, II.15.10, ed. Feenstra, p. 399, n. 10 and in *IPC*, ed. Hamaker, p. 298, n. 3, ed. Van Ittersum, p. 434, n. d.
5 Regrettably, we failed to identify Grotius's source with certainty. Our suggestion is that Grotius referred here to the works of the Athenian orator Demosthenes. He owned an edition of his orations (Molhuysen, 'De bibliotheek van Hugo de Groot', no. 325). In his manuscript work 'De iure Attico' (Leiden UL, BPL 922-II), Grotius repeatedly inserted quotations taken from Demosthenes, on the basis of the Paris edition of 1570 (ed. Jean Bienné, Jacques Dupuys and Denis Lambin). See for instance BPL 922-II, ff. 320r, 326v, 330v. Page 206 of the Paris edition of Demosthenes discusses the alliance (*συμμαχία*) between Athens and Philip II of Macedonia.
6 The reference is enigmatic: the Demosthenes edition, mentioned in the previous note, lacks columns and reading 'Col. 2 et 3' as 'Colossians chapters 2 and 3' is not very convincing. Or did Grotius have Col. 2.8; 2.18–19 and 3.11 in mind?

imminente necessitate, aliter non. Silv[ester] Bellum. 1. n. 9, concl[usio] 3. All[egat][1] Nic[olaum] de Lir[a] et alios.

Mac[cabaeorum] foedus cum Romanis. 1 Mac. 8.18. Defensivum.[2]
Rex Francisc[us].
Rex Antonius.

Ius Canonicum.

Pan[ormitanus] in c[anonem] quod super de voto: licitum esse Christ[ianis] uti auxilio Infid[elium].
All[egat][3] Oldr[adi] cons[ilia] 67.
Et all[egat] hist[oriam] Maccab[aeorum]. Item quia insidiis uti li[citum] a maiori.[4] Item quia fideles dominum infidelem licite iuvant, c[anon] Iulianus, et c[anon] si dominus, 11. Q[uaestio] 3.

1 Here, in this place, the enigmatic reference sign is more or less clearly written as: 'all' or 'alt'. Cf. *IPC*, ed. Hamaker, pp. 235, 251, 255, 270, 282, for a similar 'all'.

2 Grotius wrote this word in a scrawled hand; perhaps we should read: 'defensio'.

3 The text reads here 'all.', as in the following sentence.

4 'a maiori', sc. 'fortius' (as in Grotius's source text), meaning 'reasoned from the more extensive case'.

Sylvester on the word 'war'. 1. no. 9, conclusion 3.[1] He refers to Nicolaus de Lira and others.[2]

A treaty of the Maccabees with the Romans. 1 Mac. 8.18. Defensive.
King Francis.
King Antoine.[3]

Canon law.

Panormitanus on the canon Quod super de voto [What above on the vow]: that it is lawful for Christians to use the assistance of infidels.[4]
He refers to Oldradus's Consilia [Advices], 67.[5]
He also refers to the history of the Maccabees. Also because it is permitted to use ambushes, reasoned from the more extended case. Also because the faithful may lawfully help an unfaithful master, canon Julian, and canon Si dominus [If the owner], 11. Q[uaestio] 3.[6]

1 The quotation ('Christiani habentes ... imminente necessitate, aliter non') is taken from Sylvester Prierias, *Sylvestrinae Summae ... pars prima* (Antverpiae: Ex officina Christophori Plantini, 1569), p. 93 (left column), on 'Bellum I' ('De bello publico'), 8, concl. 3. Also cited in *IPC*, ed. Hamaker, p. 57 n. 8 and p. 298 n. 4, ed. Van Ittersum, p. 88. n. g. and p. 434, n. e, and *IBP* II.15.10.4 and II.15.11.2 (ed. Feenstra, pp. 400–401).

2 Grotius may have taken his reference to Nicolaus de Lyra from Sylvester, *Sylvestrinae Summae ... pars prima*, p. 93 (right column: concl. 3). If so, he refers to De Lyra's commentary on 1 Reg. 28.

3 Perhaps a reference to Francis I (1494–1547), king of France, or Francis II (1544–1560), king of France, and Antoine (1518–1562), king of Navarre, father of Henry IV.

4 Panormitanus, *Abbatis Panormitani ... in tertium Decretalium librum commentaria* (Venetiis: Bernardus Maiorinus, 1569), fol. 223ᵛ, 224ʳ. Cf. the reference to Panormitanus on *c. quod super de voto* [c. 8 Decretal. III, 34] in *IPC*, ed. Hamaker, p. 298, n. 3, ed. Van Ittersum, p. 434, n. d and *IBP*, II.15.10.4 (ed. Feenstra, p. 401, n. 1) and Hugo Grotius, *Observationes iuridicae contra pacem cum archiduce Alberto ineundam, non autographae*, Leiden University Library, MS BPL 922 Id, fol. 308–313 (at fol. 309ᵛ).

5 Grotius refers here to Oldradus de Ponte, *Consilia*. The text, however, is not to be found in cons. 67, but in cons. 71: 'Bellum si sit iustum Christianus potest sine peccato ad defensionem suam uti auxilio infidelium pro parte sua'. Oldradus de Ponte, *Consilia, seu responsa, et quaestiones aureae* (Venetiis: Apud Franciscum Zilettum, 1570), fol. 27. Grotius may have taken the reference to 'Oldr. cons. 67' from *Abbatis Panormitani ... in tertium Decretalium librum commentaria* (Venetiis: Bernardus Maiorinus, 1569), fol. 223ᵛ. Cf. the reference to Oldradus, cons. 71 in *IBP*, II.15.8 (ed. Feenstra, p. 395, n. 5).

6 Possibly a reference to Grat. *Decr.* C. 11, q. 3, c. 93: 'Si dominus ea iubet, quae non sunt adversa scripturis sanctis, subjiciatur servus domino,' etc. Cf. *Abbatis Panormitani ... in tertium Decretalium librum commentaria* (Venetiis: Bernardus Maiorinus, 1569), fol. 224ʳ, left column [c. 8 Decretal. III, 34]. Cf. *IBP*, II.15.10.4 (ed. Feenstra, p. 401, with a reference on p. 987 to *IPC*, fol. 142).

Iudaei Samaritanis debent officia proximi. Luc. 10.29.
Infidelitas non tollit Ius Naturale, aut humanum. Tho[mas].

Dist[inctio:] infideles ab initio. Apostolus: haereticos ab initio, sine vel cum[1] Idol[olatria];
et relapsos in haeresim. Excommunicatos, singulos, Universos.

Societas ad def[ensionem] fidelis; vel ad defensionem infidelis; vel ad off[ensionem].
Item contra fid[eles] aut contra infid[eles].

Damn[um] christianitatis aut religionis apparens: ex[2] def[ensione] aut off[ensione].

Exempla Rom[anorum] de sociis defendendis. Cic[ero]. Aug[ustinus] 3 de Civit[ate] Dei. Tho[mas].

Abraham pro Lotho arma suscipit ipse non offensus. Gen. 14.

De defendendis oppressis v[ide] al[iter][3] c[aput] 6 de Manubiis. V[ide] 23, q[uaestio] 3 per totum, praecipue c[anon] Non inferenda.

1 Reading not completely certain.
2 'ex': the reading is not certain.
3 The reading is uncertain: 'all' or 'alt'.

The Jews owe the Samaritans the duties of a neighbor. Luc. 10.29.[1]
Unbelief does not take away the natural or human law. Thomas.[2]

Distinction: unbelievers from the beginning. Apostle: heretics from the beginning, without or with idolatry; and those who have relapsed into heresy. Those who are excommunicated, individually, or in general.

Partnership for defense of the faithful; or for defense of the unbeliever; or for offense. Likewise, either against the faithful or against the unfaithful.

Evident harm to Christianity or religion: from defense or offense.

Examples of the Romans defending their allies. Cicero. Augustinus 3 The City of God. Thomas.[3]

Abraham takes up arms for Lot without being attacked himself. Gen. 14.

On the defense of the oppressed see otherwise c. 6 of De Manubiis.[4] See 23, question 3 throughout, especially canon Non inferenda [Not inflicting].[5]

---

1 Cf. the reference to Luc. 10.29 et sqq. in *IPC*, ed. Hamaker, p. 298, n. 2.

2 See *S. Th.* 2a 2ae, q. 10, a. 10, resp.: 'Ius autem divinum, quod est ex gratia, non tollit ius humanum, quod est ex naturali ratione'. Cf. the reference to *S. Th.* 2a 2ae, q. 10 a. 10 in *IBP*, II.15.8 (ed. Feenstra, p. 395, n. 3).

3 References to Cicero, Augustinus and Thomas Aquinas. See Augustine, *De civitate dei*, book 3, where Cicero is mentioned repeatedly, albeit not in the context of the duty to defend one's allies. On the other hand, book 3 includes a quotation from Sallust that relates to the matter: 'Post, ubi pericula virtute propulerant, sociis atque amicis auxilia portabant magisque dandis quam accipiendis beneficiis amicitias parabant'. Augustine concludes this quotation with a short comment: 'Decenter his artibus Roma crevit' (Aug. *Civ. Dei* 3.10).

4 We did not succeed in identifying 'c. 6 de Manubiis' with certainty. It is perhaps a reference to caput 6 of *De iure praedae*, where Grotius discusses the protection of the oppressed from injustice as one of the 'efficient causes of war.' See the introduction.

5 See Grat. *Decr.* C. 23, q. 3, c. 7, with a reference to Ambrosius 'libro de offitiis [c. 36]: Non in inferenda, sed in depellenda iniuria lex virtutis est'. Cf. *IPC*, ed. Hamaker, p. 65 n. 4.

Iudaei vetantur contra Nabuc[hodonosor] ab Aegyptio Rege auxilium petere.
Es. 31.1. et 36.6.
Sen. Ep. 95.

Iacob in Regis Aegyptii patrocinium se[1] contulit.

Ioseph, Daniel, alii in aedes barbarorum.
Esdras. Nehemias. Esther.
Esther nupta Regi profano.

2 Cor. 6.14. Nolite iugum ducere cum Infidelibus. Et seq[uentes].

Cum infidelib[us] caenare. Ita[2] 1 Cor. 10.
Exempla Christi.

Charitatis officia in o[mn]es, praecipue domesticos fidei. Gal. 6.10.
Alienigenae a[utem] foenerabis.

Commercia cum Infidelib[us]. Abr[aham] et Iacob agros[3] emunt.
Paulus tentoria vendit. Alienigenae a[utem] foenerabis.
Salomon cum Hiramo.
Contractus tenere cum infid[elibus]; leges de deditione.

Amicitia violetur vetari.

Haeretici vitandi. Tit. 3.10.

1 'se' is placed above the line.
2 This sign occurs repeatedly. Perhaps it should be explained as: 'Vi[de]'.
3 The reading 'agros' is not completely certain; possibly: 'agrem'.

The Jews are forbidden to ask the assistance of the Egyptian king against Nebuchadnezzar. Esa. 31.1 and 36.6.[1]
Seneca, Epistles, 95.[2]

Jacob committed himself to the patronage of the king of Egypt.

Joseph, Daniel, and others into the houses of barbarians.
Ezra. Nehemiah. Esther.
[right column:] Esther married to a heathen king.

2 Cor. 6.14. Avoid being yoked together with infidels. And the following.[3]

Eating with unbelievers. Thus 1 Cor. 10.[4]
Examples of Christ.

Duties of charity towards all, especially to those who are of the household of faith. Gal. 6.10.[5]
You will, however, lend to a foreigner.[6]

Trade with infidels. Abraham and Jacob buy fields.[7]
Paul sells tents.[8] You will, however, lend to a foreigner.
Solomon with Hiram.[9]
To keep contracts with the unfaithful; the laws of surrender.

To forbid that friendship is violated.

Heretics must be avoided. Tit. 3.10.

1 The eighth-century prophet Isaiah does not mention Nebuchadnezzar II (605–562 BC), king of the Neo-Babylonian Empire. Grotius assumed, however, that Isaiah had predicted events that would take place much later, during the Babylonian Captivity and the time of the Maccabees. See his annotations on Isaiah in *Opera omnia theologica* (Amsterdam: Blaeu, 1679), I, p. 308 A 18–48, 311 B 57–59, 314 A 38–39 and 330 B 59–60.
2 Sen. *Ep.* 95 ('Seneca Lucilio suo salutem. Petis a me …').
3 Grotius quoted the vulgate text. Cf. *IBP* II.15.10.3 (ed. Feenstra, p. 400).
4 1 Cor. 10.21 and 27. Cf. *IBP*, II.15.10.3 (ed. Feenstra, p. 400).
5 Cf. *IBP*, II.15.10.2 (ed. Feenstra, p. 400).
6 Deut. 15.3; 15.6; 23.19–20. See also the main text, fol. 315r.
7 Gen. 23.1–20; 33.19; Act. 7.16.
8 Act. 18.3.
9 1 Reg. 5.12.

Foedus inaequale: dedere se infidelib[us].
Ita[1] Exemplum in Iudaeis: melius servire quam interire.

316 (2)v *Right column*
Ps. 82.4: Eripite pauperem et egenum de manu peccatoris liberate.
Erue eos qui ducuntur ad mortem. Prov. 24.11.

Caiet[anus] 2. 2, q[uaestio] 40, art[iculus] 1; ibi in eodem art[iculo]: pro ultione sociorum iusta causa belli.
Item externis ministris ad bellum uti licet.

No[ta]: arg[umentum] a relatis.
Ut de usura.

συμμαχία
ἐπιμαχία
Tropheia. Foedera. Livius.
In Fabrum et Iab.[2]
De alienis subditis defendendis. V[ide] Gent[ilim].
De rebellib[us] et proditoribus.

1 Other possibilities: 'v[idemus]', 'v[ide]', or 'ite[m]'.

2 These two lines are completely incomprehensible. 'Tropheia' might also be deciphered as 'Propheta', 'Livius' as 'Civium'. Possibly the second line should be read as: 'Vi[de] Patres et I[uris]c[onsultos]'.

An unequal pact: to surrender oneself to the unfaithful.
Thus the example on the Jews: it is better to serve than to perish.[1]

6 (2)ᵛ *Right column*
Ps. 82.4:[2] Deliver the poor and liberate the needy from the hand of the sinner.
Hold back those who are being led to death. Prov. 24.11.[3]

Caietanus 2. 2. question 40, article 1; there in the same article: revenge of one's allies is a just cause of war.
Likewise, it is permissible to use foreign assistants for war.[4]

Note: Argument from related issues.
As on usury.

Defensive alliance
Offensive alliance.[5]
Trophies. Covenants. Livius.
In Fabrum and Jab.
On defending foreign subjects. See Gentili.[6]
On rebels and traitors.[7]

---

1 Ex. 14.12; cf. Hom. *Od.* 11, 488–492.

2 '82.4', read: '81.4' according to the numbering in the Vulgate.

3 Both Ps. 82 [81].4 and Prov. 24.11 are taken from the Vulgate text.

4 Cajetanus, commentary on *S. Th.* 2a 2ae, q. 40, a. 1: 'In eodem articulo circa iustitiam causae belli adverte, quod, quia amici ac socii unum censentur, ideo iusta causa indicendi bellum est pro ultione sociorum. Nec minus potest socios et extraneos ad bellum gerendum princeps invitare quam ad exercendam iustitiam intus ministros extraneos conducere' (Cajetanus, *Secunda Secundae Sancti Thomae, cum comment. Cardi. Caietani* (Lugduni: Apud Hugonem a Porta, 1548, fol. 69ᵛ)). Cf. *IBP*, I.3.5.2 (ed. Feenstra p. 97 n. 5, referring to *Caietanus in Thomam III* (Lugduni 1581), pp. 144–146, at p. 145) and II.15.10.1 (ed. Feenstra, p. 399, n. 10). Grotius may have taken the reference to Cajetanus's commentary on *S. Th.* 2a 2ae, art. 40, q. 1 from Vitoria, *De Indis*, q. 3, a. 7, § 17, to which he refers on fol. 316 (2)ᵛ, left column.

5 See also fol. 314ʳ, prem. 8.

6 Alberico Gentili, *De iure belli libri tres* (Hanoviae: Guilielmus Antonius, 1598), I.16 (pp. 118–127): 'De subditis alienis contra Dominum defendendis'.

7 Perhaps a reference to ibid., I.16, where Gentili explains that the English did right in aiding the Dutch against the Spaniards (ed. 1598, at p. 124) or III.7, where he argues that rebellion is itself the chief incentive to cruelty, and rebels and traitors should be treated more severely than (common) enemies (ed. 1598, at p. 521).

2 Cor. 7.16:
διὸ ἐξέλθατε ἐκ μέσου αὐτῶν
καὶ ἀφορίσθητε, λέγει κύριος,
καὶ ἀκαθάρτου μὴ ἅπτεσθε:
κἀγὼ εἰσδέξομαι ὑμᾶς.

Manassis affinitas cum Sanballete reprehenditur.
Neh. c[aput] 13.[28–29]; v[ide] Io[sephum].

οὐ γὰρ συγχρῶνται Ἰουδαῖοι Σαμαρίταις. Ioh. 4.9.
Christus a Sam[aritana muliere] aquam sumit.

Christus apud Pharis[aeos] caenat. Luc. 7.36 et 39.
Math. 18.17. Esto tibi ut Ethnicus et Publicanus; i[ta:] Curam tuis ne habeto: ne te scandalizent.

Inimici iuvandi tempore necessitatis. Prov. 25.21.

318v De publica societate cum infidelibus[1]

V[ide] Tract[atum] de leg[ibus] Mosaicis, p. 304.
Iunius[2] in Irenico distinguit inter inimicos Ecclesiae et amicos extra Ecclesiam.
His benefaciendum et ab his beneficia accipiend[um].
Ait:[3] qui non est quam nobis nobiscum.
Benedicentib[us] tibi benedicit de Abrahamo.

1 Grotius wrote this title in capitals.
2 From here to the end of these notes ('in ... Henrici IV') the ink is much darker (black rather than light brown). These may be notes that Grotius added at a later stage.
3 The reading of 'Ait' and the following 'quam' is uncertain. Perhaps the word 'ait' should be added to the previous sentence.

2 Cor. 7.16:[1]
come out from among them
and be absolved, says the master,
and do not touch impurity:
and I will welcome you.

Manasseh's kinship with Sanballat is criticized.
Neh. c[hapter] 13.[28–29]; see Josephus.[2]

For Jews do not mix with Samaritans. Ioh. 4.9:
Christ takes water from a Samaritan woman.[3]

Christ dines with the Pharisaeans. Luc. 7.36 and 39.
Math. 18.17. Let him be to you as a pagan and a tax-collector;[4] so: Pay no heed to your limbs: lest they offend you.[5]

Enemies should be helped in time of need. Prov. 25.21.

318v On public partnership with unbelievers.

See the Treatise on the Mosaic Laws, p. 304.[6]
Junius distinguishes in *Eirenicum* between the enemies of the Church and friends outside the Church.
The latter should be treated well and from them benefits may be accepted.
He said: there is no one with us but he who is for us.[7]
He blesses those who blessed you, on Abraham.[8]

1 Read: 2 Cor. 6.17.
2 Cf. Josephus, *Antiquitates iudaicae* XI.7.2 and XI.8.2.
3 Cf. Ioh. 4.7–10 and *IBP*, II.15.9.4 (ed. Feenstra, p. 397).
4 Grotius quoted the Vulgate text.
5 Cf. Math. 18.8–9.
6 See Wilhelmus Zepperus, *Legum mosaicarum forensium explanatio* (Herbornae Nassoviorum: Ex officina Christophori Corvini, 1604), IV.6 (at pp. 304–307): 'De federibus cum impiis et idololatris'.
7 In this enigmatic sentence, hastily jotted down, Grotius summed up Junius's description of a category of people outside the church who did not hate or damage the church, 'de quo genere dicebat Christus: Qui non est adversum nos, pro nobis est'. Cf. Franciscus Junius, *Eirenicum de pace ecclesiae catholicae* (Ludguni Batavorum: Franciscus Raphelengius, 1593), pp. 169–170, 178–179 and 174. See also Luc. 9.50 and 11.23.
8 Cf. Gen. 12.3: '... benedicam benedicentibus tibi et maledicam maledicentibus tibi ...', cited in Junius, *Eirenicum*, pp. 169–170. See also ibid., p. 179.

Qui aquam in nomine Proph[etae] ministraverint.
Math. 10.
Editum Irenicum Iunii a[nn]o 93 circa[1] mutatione[m], ut puto, Henrici IV.

1 After 'circa' Grotius deleted 'conversionem'.

Those who shall have administered water in the name of the Prophet.
Math. 10.[1]
The *Eirenicum* of Junius published in the year [15]93, I think around the change of Henry IV.[2]

1 Math. 10.41–42: 'Qui recipit prophetam nomine prophetae, mercedem prophetae accipiet, et qui recipit iustum nomine iusti, mercedem iusti accipiet. Et quicumque potum dederit uni ex his parvis poculum frigidae solum, nomine discipuli, amen dico vobis, non perdiderit mercedem suam', cited in Junius, *Eirenicum*, p. 179. In this place, Junius notes about people outside the church who treat it in a kind way: '... quos Christus pro nobis dixit esse, quandoquidem non sunt adversus nos; quibus promisit mercedem prophetae, si vas frigidae in nomine prophetae ministraverint ...'.

2 His conversion to Roman Catholicism took place on 25 July 1593.

Bibliography

Manuscripts and Archival Materials

Dutch National Archives (NA), Collectie Hugo de Groot, supplement I, access 1.10.35.02, inv. 40 (Grotius's VOC papers from the 1600s and 1610s).

Grotius, Hugo undated (ca. 1601–1602). 'De fide et perfidia,' in: *Parallelon rerumpublicarum liber tertius*, Meermanno-Westreenianum, The Hague, MS 010 E 025.

Grotius, Hugo undated (ca. 1603–1608). *Commentarius in theses XI*, Leiden University Library, MS BPL 922 Ia, fol. 276–286.

Grotius, Hugo undated (after 1604). *Theses sive quaestiones LVI*, Leiden University Library, MS BPL 922 Ib, fol. 287–290.

Grotius, Hugo undated. *Commentarius de bello ob libertatem eligendo*, Leiden University Library, MS BPL 922 Ic, fol. 293–307.

Grotius, Hugo undated (ca. 1604–1606). *De iure praedae commentarius*, Leiden University Library, MS BPL 917.

Grotius, Hugo undated (ca. 1606). Letters to the emperors of Malabar and Borneo, the kings of Siam, Johor, Ternate and Tidore, and the lords of Ambon and the Banda Islands, Dutch National Archives, The Hague, Collectie Hugo de Groot, supplement I, access 1.10.35.02, inv. 40, fol. 344–345, 359–360, 361–362, 364, 365–366, 424–425, and 430.

Grotius, Hugo undated (ca. 1606–1609). *De societate publica cum infidelibus*, Leiden University Library, MS BPL 922 Ie, fol. 314–318.

Grotius, Hugo undated (ca. 1607–1608). *De pace*, Leiden University Library, MS BPL 922 Ic, fol. 302–307.

Grotius, Hugo undated (ca. 1607–1608). *Observationes iuridicae contra pacem cum archiduce Alberto ineundam, non autographae*, Leiden University Library, MS BPL 922 Id, fol. 308–313.

Grotius, Hugo undated (ca. 1607–1608). *Vertoog opgemaakt voor de Oost-Indische Compagnie betreffende de houding, door deze bij de onderhandelingen met Spanje aan te nemen*, Dutch National Archives, The Hague, Collectie Hugo de Groot, supplement I, access 1.10.35.02, inv. 40, fol. 295–299 (first version) and 405–413 (second version).

Grotius, Hugo undated. *Ius atticum et formulae et sententiae*, Leiden University Library, MS BPL 922 II, fol. 319–347.

Grotius, Hugo undated (ca. 1613–1617). *Defensio capitis quinti maris liberi*, Leiden University Library, MS BPL 918.

Grotius, Hugo undated (ca. 1615). *Remonstrantie*, Ets Haim Library, Portuguese Synagogue, Amsterdam, MS EH 48 A 02.

Primary Sources

Aquinas, Thomas 1612. *Secunda secundae D. Thomae de Aquino*, Venetiis: Apud Iuntas.

Aquinas, Thomas 1916 (ca. 1265). *Summa Theologiae of St. Thomas Aquinas*, trans. Fathers of the English Dominican Province (Lawrence Shapcote), London: Burns, Oates and Washbourne.

Aquinas, Thomas 1970 (ca. 1256). *Liber contra impugnantes Dei cultum et religionem*, ed. H.F. Dondaine (Leonina), Romae: Ad Sanctae Sabinae.

Arias, Franciscus 1584. *De bello et eius iustitia*, in: *Tractatus illustrium ... iurisconsultorum*, Venetiis: Apud Franciscum Zilettum.

Aristotle 1934. *The Nicomachean Ethics*, trans. H. Rackham, Cambridge, MA: Harvard University Press (Loeb Classical Library).

Augustine, Aurelius 1957–1972. *The City of God against the Pagans*, ed. George Englert MacCracken, Cambridge, MA: Harvard University Press (Loeb Classical Library).

Augustine, Aurelius 1971. *Expositio quarundam propositionum ex epistola ad Romanos; epistolae ad Galatas expositionis liber unus ...*, ed. Johannes Divjak, Vindobonae: Hoelder-Pichler-Tempsky.

Cajetanus, Thomas de Vio 1548. *Secunda Secundae Sancti Thomae, cum comment. Cardi. Caietani*, Lugduni: Apud Hugonem a Porta.

Cau, Cornelis 1658. *Groot Placaet-Boeck vervattende de placaten, ordonnantien en edicten van de doorluchtige, Hoogh Moghende Heeren Staten-Generael der Vereenighde Nederlanden*, 's Gravenhage: Van Wouw.

Cicero 1913. *De officiis*, trans. Walter Miller, Cambridge, MA: Harvard University Press (Loeb Classical Library).

Cicero 1928. *De re publica*, trans. Clinton Walker Keyes, Cambridge, MA: Harvard University Press (Loeb Classical Library).

Cicero 1935. *Pro Plancio*, trans. Neville Watts, Cambridge, MA: Harvard University Press (Loeb Classical Library).

Cicero 2014. *De amicitia*, trans. William Armistead Falconer, Cambridge, MA: Harvard University Press (Loeb Classical Library).

Diogenes Laertius 1925. *Lives of Eminent Philosophers*, trans. Robert Drew Hicks, Cambridge, MA: Harvard University Press (Loeb Classical Library).

Gellius, Aulus 1928. *The Attic Nights of Aulus Gellius*, trans. John C. Rolfe, London: Heinemann (Loeb Classical Library).

Gentili, Alberico 1598. *De iure belli libri tres*, Hanoviae: Guilielmus Antonius.

Gentili, Alberico 1933 (1612). *De iure belli libri tres*, reproduction and English translation of the 1612 edition, trans. John C. Rolfe and introd. Coleman Phillipson, Oxford: Clarendon.

Gratian 1959 (ca. 1140). *Decretum Gratiani*, in: *Corpus iuris canonici*, ed. Friedberg, Graz: Akademische Druck- und Verlagsanstalt.

Gregorius IX 1582. *Decretales D. Gregorii Papae IX una cum glossis restitutae*, Roma: In aedibus populi Romani.

Grotius, Hugo 1609. *Mare liberum*, Lugduni Batavorum: Ex officina Ludovici Elzevirii.

Grotius, Hugo 1625. *De iure belli ac pacis libri tres*, Parisiis: Apud Nicolaum Buon.

Grotius, Hugo 1629 (1627). *De veritate religionis Christianae*, Lugduni Batavorum: Ex officina Ioannis Maire.

Grotius, Hugo 1658. *Annales et historiae de rebus Belgicis*, Amstelaedami: Ex typographeio Joannis Blaeu.

Grotius, Hugo 1679. *Opera omnia theologica*, Amstelaedami: Apud heredes Joannis Blaeu.

Grotius, Hugo 1720 (1645). *De iure belli ac pacis libri tres*, ed. Johannes Gronovius, Amstelaedami: Ex officina Wetsteniana.

Grotius, Hugo 1868 (ca. 1604). *De iure praedae commentarius*, ed. H.G. Hamaker, The Hague: Martinus Nijhoff.

Grotius, Hugo 1925. *Briefwisseling*, ed. P.C. Molhuysen, The Hague: Martinus Nijhoff.

Grotius, Hugo 1925 (1646). *De jure belli ac pacis libri tres*, ed. James Brown Scott, trans. Francis W. Kelsey (Oxford: Clarendon Press).

Grotius, Hugo 1993 (1625 and later editions). *De iure belli ac pacis libri tres*, ed. B.J.A de Kanter-Van Hettinga Tromp, annot. F. Feenstra, C.E. Persenaire, and E. Arps-de Wilde, Aalen: Scientia Verlag.

Grotius, Hugo 2006 (ca. 1604). *Commentary on the Law of Prize and Booty*, ed. and introd. Martine van Ittersum, trans. Gwladys L. Williams, Indianapolis: Liberty Fund.

Grotius, Hugo 2009 (1609). *Mare liberum, 1609–2009*, Latin text and English translation, ed. R. Feenstra and J. Vervliet, trans. Gwladys L. Williams, Leiden: Brill.

Grotius, Hugo 2015 (ca. 1601–1602). 'De fide et perfidia,' Latin text and English translation, trans. and introd. Arthur Eyffinger, *Grotiana* 36, 79–171.

Grotius, Hugo 2019 (1615). *Remonstrantie of 1615: Facsimile, Transliteration, Modern Translations and Analysis*, ed. David Kromhout and Adri K. Offenberg, trans. Cis van Heerum, Leiden: Brill.

Heeres, J.E. and F.W. Stapel (eds.) 1907–1955. *Corpus diplomaticum Neerlando-Indicum: Verzameling van politieke contracten en verdere verdragen door de Nederlanders in het Oosten gesloten* ..., The Hague: Martinus Nijhoff, 6 vols.

Josephus 1937. *Jewish Antiquities*, ed. Ralph Marcus, MA: Harvard University Press (Loeb Classical Library).

Junius, Franciscus 1593. *Eirenicum de pace ecclesiae catholicae*, Ludguni Batavorum: Franciscus Raphelengius.

Justinian 1551. *Institutiones imperatoris semper maximi divi Iustiniani*, Lugduni: Apud Hugonem a Porta, & Antonium Vincentium.

Justinian 1572. *Codicis DN. Iustiniani*, Lugduni: Apud Hugonem a Porta.

Justinian 1572. *Digestum vetus, seu Pandectarum iuris civilis*, Lugduni: Apud Hugonem a Porta.

Justinian 1998 (ca. 532). *The Digest of Justinian*, trans. Alan Watson, Philadelphia: University of Philadelphia Press, 4 vols.

Juvenal 2014. *Satires*, trans. Susanna Morton Braund, Cambridge MA: Harvard University Press (Loeb Classical Library).

Langius, Josephus 1605. *Loci communes sive florilegium rerum et materiarum selectarum ... ex Sacris Litteris ...*, Argentorati: Iosias Rihelius.

Livy 1919. *History of Rome*, trans. B.O. Foster, Cambridge, MA: Harvard University Press (Loeb Classical Library).

Marloratus, Augustinus 1601. *Propheticae et apostolicae, id est totius divinae ac canonicae Scripturae thesaurus in locos communes ... digestus*, ed. Guil. Feuguerius, Bern: Ioannes Le Preux.

Molina, Luis de 1594. *De iustitia*, Venetiis: Apud minimam societatem.

Oldradus de Ponte 1570. *Consilia, seu responsa & quaestiones aureae*, Venetiis: Apud Franciscum Zilettum.

Panormitanus 1569. *Abbatis Panormitani ... in tertium Decretalium librum commentaria*, Venetiis: Bernardus Maiorinus.

Prierias, Sylvester 1569. *Sylvestrinae Summae ... pars prima*, Antverpiae: Ex officina Christophori Plantini.

Scaliger, Josephus Justus 1606. *Thesaurus temporum*, Leiden: Basson and Commelinus.

Scaliger, Josephus Justus 1606. *Animadversiones in Chronologica Eusebii*, Leiden: Basson and Commelinus.

Seneca 1925. *Epistles*, trans. Richard M. Gummere, Cambridge MA: Harvard University Press (Loeb Classical Library).

Seneca 1935. *De beneficiis*, trans. John William Basore, Cambridge MA: Harvard University Press (Loeb Classical Library).

Soto, Domingo de 1566. *Deliberatio in causa pauperum*, Salamanca: Ioannes Maria a Terranova.

Suarez, Francisco 1944. *Selections from Three Works of Francisco Suarez*, trans. Gwladys L. Williams, Ammi Brown and John Waldron, Oxford: Clarendon Press, vol. 2.

Theodosius II 1952. *The Theodosian Code and Novels and the Sirmondian Constitutions: A Translation with Commentary, Glossary, and Bibliography*, ed. and trans. Clyde Pharr, in collaboration with Theresa Sherrer Davidson and Mary Brown Pharr, introd. C. Dickerman Williams, Princeton: Princeton University Press.

Thucydides 1919. *History of the Peloponnesian War*, trans. C.F. Smith, Cambridge MA: Harvard University Press (Loeb Classical Library).

Tremellius, Immanuel and Franciscus Junius 1603. *Testamenti Veteris Biblia Sacra*, Hanau: Typis Wechelianis, apud Claudium Marnium et haeredes Joannis Aubrii.

Vitoria, Francisco de 1557. 'De Indis insulanis relectio prior,' in: *Relectiones theologicae XII*, Lugduni: Apud Iacobum Boyerium.

Vitoria, Francisco de 1557. 'De potestate civili,' in: *Relectiones theologicae XII*, Lugduni: Apud Iacobum Boyerium.

Vitoria, Francisco de 2010. *Political Writings*, ed. and trans. Anthony Pagden and Jeremy Lawrance, Cambridge: Cambridge University Press, 231–292.

Zepperus, Wilhelmus 1604. *Legum mosaicarum forensium explanation*, Herbornae Nassoviorum: Ex officina Christophori Corvini.

Secondary Sources

Aroney, N. 2016. 'Subsidiarity, Federalism, and the Best Constitution: Thomas Aquinas on City, Province and Empire,' in: *Aquinas and Modern Law*, R. Brooks and J. Murphy eds., Abingdon.

Asmis, E. 2004. 'The State as Partnership: Cicero's Definition of Res Publica in his Work on the State,' *History of Political Thought* 25, 569–599.

Blom, H. 2014. 'The Meaning of Trust: *Fides* between Self-Interest and *Appetitus Societatis*,' in: *The Roots of International Law/ Les fondements du droit international: Liber Amicorum Peter Haggenmacher*, P.-M. Dupuy and V. Chetail eds., Leiden, 39–58.

Blom, H. 2015. 'Sociability and Hugo Grotius,' *History of European Ideas* 41, 589–604.

Blom, H. 2018. 'Hugo Grotius on Trust: Its Causes and Effects,' in: *Trust and Happiness in the History of Political Thought*, L. Kontler and M. Somos eds., Leiden, 76–98.

Borschberg, P. 1994. *Hugo Grotius' Commentarius in Theses XI: An Early Treatise on Sovereignty, the Just War, and the Legitimacy of the Dutch Revolt*, Bern.

Borschberg, P. 1996. 'De Pace: Ein unveröffentlichtes Fragment von Hugo Grotius über Krieg und Frieden,' *Zeitschrift der Savigny-Stiftung für Rechtsgeschichte: Romanistische Abteilung* 113, 268–292.

Borschberg, P. 1998. 'De societate publica cum infidelibus: Ein Frühwerk von Hugo Grotius', *Zeitschrift der Savigny-Stiftung für Rechtsgeschichte: Romanistische Abteilung* 115, 355–393.

Borschberg, P. 2006/7. 'Grotius, the Social Contract, and Political Resistance: A Study of the Unpublished Theses LVI,' *International Law and Justice Working Papers*, 1–87.

Borschberg, P. 2011. *Hugo Grotius, the Portuguese and Free Trade in the East Indies*, Singapore.

Borschberg, P. 2020. 'Cornelis Matelief, Hugo Grotius, and the King of Siam (1605–1616): Agency, Initiative and Diplomacy,' *Modern Asian Studies* 54, 123–156.

Borschberg, P. 2021. 'Hugo Grotius and the East Indies,' in: *The Cambridge Companion to Hugo Grotius*, R. Lesaffer and J. Nijman eds., Cambridge, 65–90.

Brett, A. 2011. *Changes of State: Nature and the Limits of the City in Early Modern Natural Law*, Cambridge, 11–36.

Clayton L.A. and D.M. Lantigua 2020. *Bartolomé de las Casas and the Defense of Amerindian Rights: A Brief History with Documents*, Tuscaloosa.

Condorelli, O. 2020. 'Grotius's Doctrine of Alliances with Infidels and the Idea of *Respublica Christiana*,' *Grotiana* 41, 13–39.

Eysinga, W.J.M. van & L.J. Noordhoff (eds.) 1952 (1864). *Catalogue de manuscrits autographs de Hugo Grotius dont la vente a eu lieu à la Haye le 15 novembre 1864 sous la direction et au domicile de Martinus Nijhoff*, The Hague.

Eysinga, W.J.M. van 1958. 'Eene onuitgegeven nota van De Groot', in: *Sparsa collecta: Een aantal der verspreide geschriften van Jonkheer Mr. W.J.M. van Eysinga*, F.M. van Asbeck, E.N. van Kleffens, K.P. van der Mandele en J.R. Stellinga eds., Leiden, 488–504.

Fikentscher, W. 1979. *De Fide et Perfidia: Der Treuegedanke in den Staatsparallelen des Hugo Grotius aus heutiger Sicht*, Munich.

Fruin, R. 1925. 'An Unpublished Work of Hugo Grotius,' *Bibliotheca Visseriana* 5, 3–71.

Garnier, É. 2008. *L'alliance impie: François 1er et Soliman le Magnifique contre Charles v*, Paris.

Haggenmacher, H. 1983. *Grotius et la doctrine de la guerre juste*, Paris.

Hulle, I. van 2016. 'Grotius, Informal Empire and the Conclusion of Unequal Treaties,' *Grotiana* 37, 43–60.

Ittersum, M. van 2006. *Profit and Principle: Hugo Grotius, Natural Rights Theories and the Rise of Dutch Power in the East Indies (1595–1615)*, Leiden.

Ittersum, M. van 2006–2007. 'Preparing *Mare liberum* for the Press: Hugo Grotius' Rewriting of Chapter 12 of *De iure praedae* in November–December 1608,' *Grotiana* 26–28, 246–280.

Ittersum, M. van 2009. 'Dating the Manuscript of *De jure praedae* (1604–1608): What Watermarks, Foliation, and Quire Divisions Can Tell Us About Hugo Grotius's Development as a Natural Rights and Natural Law Theorist,' *History of European Ideas* 35, 125–193.

Ittersum, M. van 2010. 'The Long Goodbye: Hugo Grotius' Justification of Dutch Expansion Overseas,' *History of European Ideas* 36, 386–411.

Ittersum, M. van 2016. 'Confiscated Books and Manuscripts: What Happened to the Personal Library and Archive of Hugo Grotius Following his Arrest on Charges of High Treason in August 1618?', in: *Lost Books: Reconstructing the Print World of Pre-Industrial Europe*, Flavia Bruni and Andrew Pettegree eds., Leiden, 362–385.

Ittersum, M. van 2024. *The Working Papers of Hugo Grotius: Transmission, Dispersal and Loss, 1604–1884*, Leiden.

Kaser, M. 1975. *Das römische Privatrecht*, Munich.

Keene, E. 2002. *Beyond the Anarchical Society: Grotius, Colonialism and Order in World Politics*, Cambridge.

Kunkel, W. 1966. *Roman Legal and Constitutional History*, trans. J.M. Kelly, Oxford.

Lantigua, D.M. 2020. *Infidels and Empires in a New World Order: Early Modern Spanish Contributions to International Legal Thought*, Cambridge.

Laurentius, Th. and F. 2007. *Watermarks 1600–1650 Found in the Zeeland Archives*, Houten.

Lesaffer, R. 2020. 'Grotius on Reprisal,' *Grotiana* 41, 330–348.

Lesaffer, R. 2021. 'The Laws of War- and Peace-Making,' in: *The Cambridge Companion to Hugo Grotius*, R. Lesaffer and Janne Nijman eds., Cambridge, 433–456.

Lesaffer R. and J. Nijman (eds.) 2021. *The Cambridge Companion to Hugo Grotius*, Cambridge.

McGrade, A., J. Kilcullen and M. Kempshall (eds.) 2011. *The Cambridge Translations of Medieval Philosophical Texts*, Cambridge.

Molhuysen, P.C. 1943. 'De bibliotheek van Hugo de Groot in 1618', *Mededeelingen der Koninklijke Nederlandsche Akademie der Wetenschappen, Afdeeling Letteren, nieuwe serie* 6 (3), Amsterdam.

Moll, G. 1902. 'De confiscatie der goederen van Hugo de Groot,' *Oud Holland* 20 (2), 83–112.

Nellen, H. 2011. 'Hugo Grotius over kaapvaart en commerciële expansie,' *Leidschrift* 26, 59–73.

Nellen, H. 2017. *Hugo Grotius: A Lifelong Struggle for Peace in Church and State, 1583–1645*, Leiden.

Nellen, H. 2021. *Geen vredestichter is zonder tegensprekers: Hugo de Groot: Geleerde, staatsman, verguisd verzoener*, Amsterdam.

Nicholas, B. 1975. *An Introduction to Roman Law*, Oxford.

Nifterik, G. van 2001. 'Hugo Grotius on Slavery,' *Grotiana* 22, 233–243.

Nifterik, G. van 2021. 'Arguments Related to Slavery in Seventeenth-Century Dutch Legal Theory', *Tijdschrift voor Rechtsgeschiedenis* 89 (1–2), 158–191.

Noordhoff, L.J. 1953. *Beschrijving van het zich in Nederland bevindende en nog onbeschreven gedeelte der papieren afkomstig van Huig de Groot welke in 1864 zijn geveild*, Groningen.

Schröder, P. 2021. 'Trust (*fides*),' in: *The Cambridge Companion to Hugo Grotius*, R. Lesaffer and J. Nijman eds., Cambridge, 118–137.

Smelt, W.E. 1928. 'Beschrijving eener verzameling papieren, afkomstig van Hugo de Groot,' *Inventarissen van Rijks- en andere archieven*, The Hague.

Straumann, B. 2003–2004. 'Oikeiosis and appetitus societatis: Hugo Grotius' Ciceronian Argument for Natural Law and Just War,' *Grotiana* 24–25, 41–66.

Straumann, B. 2009. 'Is Modern Liberty Ancient? Roman Remedies and Natural Rights in Hugo Grotius's Early Works on Natural Law,' *Law and History Review* 27, 55–86.

Straumann, B. 2019. *Roman Law in the State of Nature: The Classical Foundations of Hugo Grotius's Natural Law*, trans. B. Cooper, Cambridge.

Todeschini, G. 2010. 'The Incivility of Judas: "Manifest" Usury as a Metaphor for the "Infamy of Fact" (*infamia facti*),' in: *Money, Morality, and Culture in Late Medieval and Early Modern Europe*, D. Wolfthal and J. Vitullo eds., London.

Tuck, R. 2012. 'Alliances with Infidels in the European Imperial Expansion,' in: *Empire and Modern Political Thought*, ed. S. Muthu, Cambridge, 61–83.

Wilde, M. de 2011. '*Fides publica* in Ancient Rome and its Reception by Grotius and Locke,' *Tijdschrift voor rechtsgeschiedenis* 79, 455–487.

Wilde, M. de 2017. 'Offering Hospitality to Strangers: Hugo Grotius's Draft Regulations for the Jews', *Tijdschrift voor Rechtsgeschiedenis* 85, 391–433.

Wilde, M. de 2020. 'Hugo Grotius's *De Societate publica cum infidelibus*: Justifying Overseas Expansionism or Religious Toleration,' *Tijdschrift voor rechtsgeschiedenis* 88, 422–439.

Wilde, M. de 2022. 'Allying with Unbelievers: Hugo Grotius's Letters to East-Indian Rulers,' *Journal of the History of International Law* 25, 1–35.

Wilde, M. de 2024. 'Protecting Non-Christian Allies: Hugo Grotius's Justification of Dutch Overseas Expansion,' in: *Avant l'état: Droit international et pluralisme politico-juridique en Europe, XIIIe–XVIIe siècle*, D. Fedele, R. Lesaffer and P. Savy eds., Rome, 269–289.

Wilson, E. 2008. *Savage Republic: De Indis of Hugo Grotius, Republicanism and Dutch Hegemony within the Early-Modern World System (c. 1600–1619)*, Leiden.

Winkel, L. 2000. 'Les origines antiques de l'appetitus societatis de Grotius,' *Tijdschrift voor rechtsgeschiedenis* 68, 393–403.

Winkel, L. 2005–2007. 'Problems of Legal Systematization from *De iure praedae* to *De iure belli ac pacis*,' *Grotiana* 26–28, 61–78.

IJsewijn, J. and D. Sacré 1998. *Companion to Neo-Latin Studies, Part II: Literary, Linguistic and Editorial Questions*, Leuven: Leuven University Press.

Index Locorum

1 Fontes Iuris

2 Fontes Antiqui

3 Fontes Biblici

Vetus Testamentum

General Index

www.ingramcontent.com/pod-product-compliance
Lightning Source LLC
Chambersburg PA
CBHW071346230926
51846CB00002B/458
9789004744585